STOP HER

A manual to help sufferers u[nderstand and]
show what can be done t[o...]

STOP HERPES NOW!

by

**Barbara B. North PhD, MD
and Penelope P. Crittenden**

THORSONS PUBLISHERS LIMITED
Wellingborough, Northamptonshire

First published 1985

© BARBARA B. NORTH and PENELOPE P. CRITTENDEN
1985

This book is sold subject to the condition that it shall not, by way of trade or otherwise, be lent, re-sold, hired out, or otherwise circulated without the publisher's prior consent in any form of binding or cover other than that in which it is published and without a similar condition including this condition being imposed on the subsequent purchaser.

British Library Cataloguing in Publication Data

North, Barbara B.
   Stop herpes now!
   1. Herpes simplex
   I. Title   II. Crittenden, Penelope P.
616.5'2   RC147.H6

ISBN 0-7225-0954-5

Printed and bound in Great Britain
by Richard Clay (The Chaucer Press) Ltd, Bungay, Suffolk

CONTENTS

	Page
Introduction	7
Chapter	
1. Life of the Herpes Virus	9
2. What If I Get Herpes?	16
3. What Does Nutrition Have To Do With Herpes?	23
4. Suppress Herpes – Lysine and Arginine	31
5. Stop Your Herpes with Stress Management	43
6. When You Get an Attack	54
7. Prevention and Protection	62
8. Another Approach to Herpes	68
9. Interviews	75
10. Questions and Answers	87
11. The Herpes Handbook	99
Appendix	103
References	105
Index	109

INTRODUCTION

But There's No Cure for Herpes Is There?
No, there is no known cure for herpes yet. There is still no injection or pill or medication of any kind that you can take to cure your case of herpes permanently. But this doesn't mean you can't do anything about your herpes infection. There are many things you can do to help prevent herpes attacks, or to clear up an attack more quickly. We have written this book to help you gain control over herpes, to demystify the subject of herpes, to help you understand exactly what herpes is, and, most of all, to show you what you can do about it.

In this day and age we are so used to being able to cure diseases that we naturally become frightened when we contract something that is labelled 'incurable' by the medical profession. However, incurable doesn't necessarily mean uncontrollable. The common cold is a good example. We all know that there is no 'cure' for a cold. But we also know various ways to avoid catching one and what steps to take if we do catch one. Herpes is no different from the common cold. It is contagious, very common, can occur over and over, can be mild or severe, rare in your life or frequent. What we are learning is that the frequency and severity of herpes attacks – like colds – depend in large measure on you.

In the next few chapters we will explain exactly what herpes is and how it infects its human host. You will learn about the two most frequent types of herpes infections and how to know if you have herpes. You will learn when herpes can be dangerous and what to do about these times. You will learn how to avoid herpes. The more information you have, the safer you will be. Most important, you will learn how you can control the frequency and severity of your herpes attacks – actual techniques you can use to keep herpes to a minimum. Contracting herpes can be a devastating experience – but it doesn't have to be. Armed with information and common sense, one can gain such control over herpes as to render it merely an inconvenience – much like the common cold.

1.
LIFE OF THE HERPES VIRUS

Herpes is a specific kind of micro-organism called a virus. Viruses are extremely small, usually smaller than bacteria. Some scientists don't even consider them to be truly living creatures because they can't survive on their own. In order to exist, viruses have to be inside the living cells of another organism. The life-span of a herpes virus outside of the human body is only a matter of hours. Human herpes viruses constitute a group of related viruses which cause several ailments: CMV (cytomegalovirus), an illness which resembles mononucleosis; VZV (varicella zoster virus), often called shingles or herpes zoster*; and HSV (herpes simplex virus), the 'common' herpes. It is HSV that is responsible for the two most common types of herpes infection: herpes simplex type 1 (generally the cause of cold sores around the mouth and lips), and herpes simplex type 2 (primarily responsible for genital herpes). It is these two viruses with which we will concern ourselves.

The herpes virus has a very simple design. It consists of a central core of genetic material (called DNA), a surrounding layer of proteins and an outer membrane. In order for the herpes virus to infect human skin, it must work its way inside the surface skin cells. It does this best when skin cells are soft and moist. Once inside, it uses its own genetic material to take control of the cell's activities.

* See more about herpes zoster in Chapter 10, Questions and Answers.

It then begins to direct those cells to manufacture more duplicate viruses. This process is analogous to the following: your cells are like a well-equipped manufacturing plant. Each one contains plenty of raw materials, tools, water, power, and skilled workers to run the plant. Assume your plant is set up to manufacture lawn-mowers. However, all it would take to manufacture mopeds is a change in management: the right equipment is already there. A new manager comes in and says, 'Now we're going to manufacture mopeds' and the plant that produced lawn mowers yesterday puts out mopeds today. That is precisely what a herpes virus does – it changes the instructions to your cells. Once the virus takes over, it can supervise the construction of many new viruses in a single cell. Soon the cell dies, breaks open and spews out the new viruses which infect neighbouring cells. These infected and broken cells form the 'cold sores' around the mouth (herpes 1) and the sores around the genitals (herpes 2).

The newly produced herpes viruses become concentrated in the sores during an attack and are very infectious. However, in order to move from person to person, the virus has to be transferred from skin to skin in a relatively moist state. The virus is actually quite delicate and cannot survive for more than a few hours without moisture. In one series of experiments, herpes researchers found that herpes viruses taken from fresh sores were able to survive for a few hours on wood, cloth, or metal surfaces. That is, when the virus was placed on wood or metal, then returned later to a test tube containing everything needed for growth, some of the viruses survived. However, most experts feel that this does not mean that the herpes virus can sit around on dry surfaces for hours and still be very contagious. It is easier for a virus to infect the 'ideal' contents of a test tube than human tissue.[1]

After a herpes attack runs its course, the virus retreats into a dormant stage. In this stage it does not leave the body; instead it migrates deeper into the body, away from the skin. Most researchers believe that the virus actually hibernates in clusters of nerve cells called ganglia.[2,3,4,5] Herpes type 1 (around the mouth) hibernate in ganglia located in the neck, and the herpes type 2 (genital) probably stay in ganglia found in the pelvis.

In some people, the hibernating herpes virus seems to stay dormant indefinitely. In others, it becomes periodically reactivated, migrating from its ganglia out to the skin to begin duplicating which causes another attack of contagious skin sores. The factors that trigger a recurrent attack depend on the individual. However, some trigger factors are very common. Any kind of significant stress may increase the likelihood of recurrence. This can be an emotional stress or a physical stress (such as illness, fatigue, poor diet, surgery, fever). Someone who has experienced repeated attacks can often tell you exactly what he or she has done to bring it on. 'I got a cold and didn't take care of myself . . . and I knew I would get an attack.' 'I always get an attack around my vacation probably because I eat badly, and travel is very hard on me.'

> Sam E. had had herpes for years, and he knew how to control it by monitoring his diet and keeping his stress level down. Sam was perplexed because one summer he had repeated outbreaks. We asked Sam what was different about his life that summer. Sam thought. Suddenly a light dawned. 'My wife's mother visited us. We all get along fine, so there aren't any unusual problems with emotional stress. But what did happen was she took the downstairs bedroom where we usually sleep and Marge and I moved upstairs. I don't really sleep well in the upstairs bed. I was simply short of sleep.'

This type of stress-producing factor will increase the chances of activating your herpes because stress damages your body's defences by suppressing your immune system.

This system is a delicately balanced network of protein antibodies, white blood cells, and specialized internal organs (like the spleen and lymph nodes) which work to entrap, neutralize or destroy invading germs – bacteria and viruses. Almost any kind of physical, mental or emotional stress can interfere with the normal function of your immune system. So anything that is hard on our minds or our bodies is hard on our immune system as well. And when our immune system is not in peak condition, the chances of a herpes outbreak increase. The herpes virus is not independent of the body which it occupies. How we treat that body has a great deal to do with how often herpes will reoccur. We can exert a great deal of control over our reactions to stress.

Who Gets Herpes?

Who is likely to get herpes? The answer is: almost anyone. Some experts estimate that 50 per cent to 90 per cent of the adult population of the entire world is afflicted with herpes type 1, which usually causes the painful skin sores around the mouth and lips.[6] Type 2, which usually causes sores in the genital region, is catching up fast. Perhaps 3 per cent of sexually active adults have herpes 2, and there are several million new cases each year.[5] No wonder people are alarmed. This is truly an epidemic and a legitimate cause for concern. Let's look at how the two types are usually contracted.

Herpes around the mouth – commonly called cold sores or fever blisters or canker sores – is the most common recurrent herpes infection and is usually caused by type 1. Type 1 herpes infections probably develop, in most people, during childhood: at family get-togethers or with the usual kissing and touching that occurs in normal socializing. Aunt Sarah kisses little Willie; possibly Uncle John gives Edna a bit of his cake. Keep in mind that herpes travels best in a moist environment. Sometimes the herpes will show up two to fourteen days after contact. Other times the infection becomes latent and only recurs during particularly stressful times – times which enable the virus to become active and grow and produce new sores.

An attack begins with a burning or tingling sensation in or near the lips. Then one or more small, round blisters (called vesicles) filled with clear fluid may appear. These vesicles soon burst, leaving a shallow, red, often painful ulcer. After seven to fourteen days the ulcers crust over and heal. Herpes is extremely contagious when the sores are present. The fluid they contain is packed with newly-produced viruses. Many people with herpes around the mouth report that stress, fatigue, injury, eating arginine-rich foods (seeds, nuts, chocolate), sun exposure, and fever, are events which commonly trigger an attack.

Herpes type 2 usually occurs around the genitals. The first attack may occur from two to fourteen days after intimate contact with the fluid from open herpes sores. The mucosal tissue around the genitals is highly susceptible to infection. So much so that the sores needn't be open to transmit the herpes virus. The presence of the sores *in any stage* is enough to pass the virus from one person to another. The fluid-filled vesicles appear first, then burst, leaving red painful ulcers. Some sufferers report that most of the tenderness occurs before the blisters actually break. After they break, crusting and healing usually takes five to twelve days, although a severe attack may last longer.

In women, herpes sores are usually located on the moist labia or near the anus. Occasionally sores will occur on the buttocks. Very rarely a sore may appear inside the vagina or on the cervix (the base of the uterus at the end of the vagina). Sometimes, sores are found in the tube which empties the bladder (the urethra). This can be very painful and may interfere with urination. Most sores, however, are located on and around the labia and can easily be seen. Women often describe itching, burning or tingling at the place where the herpes sore later appears. Some also experience pain in the legs or buttocks, or a vaginal discharge during an attack. Other symptoms include swelling and tenderness in the lymph nodes located in the groin area, a mild fever, headache and generally feeling unwell.

Herpes in men usually appears somewhere on the penis. The number of sores ranges from one to eight. As with women, sores may be found on the buttocks and near the anus. Rarely, they will be found in the urethra, causing a discharge and painful urination. Low-grade fever, general malaise and swollen lymph nodes in the groin may also occur in men.

Regardless of the location of the herpes attack, the 'primary' episode is usually the worst. Repeat attacks are almost always milder, less painful, have fewer sores and heal faster. Statistically, many people do have recurrences; however, don't just assume you will be one of them. This statistic applies to people who have not taken any steps to control and prevent repeated attacks. So when you begin to get serious about taking care of yourself, you can expect to beat the statistics.

When Is Herpes Contagious?

This is one of the most important questions people ask. You can be certain that a person is very contagious when the herpes sores are actually present – especially during the first few days. An individual can continue to be contagious for several days after the sores are healed.[7] A rule of thumb would be to avoid any interpersonal contact from the minute you suspect that an attack may be starting (tingling, burning, itching) until at least a week after the sores have disappeared. Some researchers feel that the existing herpes virus can also be shed from the body even when no attack has recently occurred.[8,9] The risk of acquiring herpes at such times has not been proven and is, in all probability, quite small.

The location of a herpes sore doesn't always tell you what type it is. Generally, type 1 is around the mouth and type 2 in the genital area. But this is not always the case. One study found that about 15 per cent of cases of genital herpes were caused by type 1 and that these cases were much less likely to recur than genital herpes caused by type 2.[10] It looks as though type 1 can be communiated from the area around the mouth to the genital area – at least in some cases. Experts believe that an increase in oral sex may be responsible for this. Also, it may be possible for an individual to accidentally take live type 1 virus from a mouth sore and transfer it to the genital region with moist fingers or even damp towels or face-cloths. This can happen to anyone – children or adults.

But don't be unduly alarmed; it is not necessary to ban the herpes sufferer from the society of others, or to burn clothing, break dishes or exercise other extreme measures. Experts feel that there is little risk of spreading herpes in this way if you simply use common sense. Treat herpes like any other contagious condition, a cold for example. Use basic personal hygiene to prevent its spread. When herpes is present, wash hands after touching areas near sores, avoid touching the sores, don't share towels, clothing, utensils, tooth brushes, avoid social kissing and sexual intimacy.

2.
WHAT IF I GET HERPES?

If you suspect that you may have acquired herpes, it is best to go to a health professional who is accustomed to dealing with herpes. Have your sores diagnosed correctly so they can be treated properly. If you go to your doctor as soon as you develop a sore (try to get in within a day or two) he or she may be able to tell you whether or not you have herpes just by examining the sore – usually with about 90 per cent certainty. Don't go in before you have a sore even if you are quite certain you have been in contact with someone who has herpes because it simply cannot be diagnosed unless the sore is actually present.

If you want to be even more certain about the diagnosis, you may ask for a test called a herpes culture. This is a simple procedure where the doctor takes a sample of the fluid from the suspected sore (using a cotton-tipped swab) and quickly places it in a special liquid. It is then transported to a virus laboratory where they take the liquid sample and inoculate it into a glass container which contains some living cells (originally taken from some kind of mammal) and a fluid which supplies all the nutrients needed to keep the cells healthy and reproducing (something like serum). This is called a culture. If the liquid taken from the sore contains herpes virus, the virus will infect the living cells in the culture and begin to reproduce – just as it does in the human body. Once it increases in number, it can be easily detected. This culture procedure typically takes several days. However, there are new methods being developed that may take less than twenty-four hours.

These culture tests are very reliable and can give you a more definite answer about whether or not you have herpes. However, they aren't perfect, and a negative result may occur because the sample wasn't taken soon enough or was not handled properly by the laboratory. However, a positive result makes it pretty certain you do have herpes – with 95 per cent to 98 per cent accuracy. Very few are missed by the culture method. The only real disadvantage of the herpes culture test is that it is relatively expensive.

Other tests can be used to diagnose herpes, but they are not reliable. Probably the most common is the Pap smear in women. The Pap smear is a simple test developed by a physician named Papanicolaou. It was originally designed to detect cervical cancer in its earlier stages. Papanicolaou found that if a few cells are gently removed from the surface of the cervix and examined under the microscope, one can see changes in the appearance of the cells that are the early warning signs of cancer. The smear is easily obtained by gently scraping the surface of the cervix with a flat piece of wood that resembles a tongue depressor.

Sometimes cells on the Pap smear will also show signs that they have been infected with herpes virus. If your Pap report says you may have herpes, there is a reasonable chance that you do. However, if there is no indication of herpes on your Pap smear, it isn't much help. Over 40 per cent of herpes infections are missed on the Pap smear.

Complications From Herpes

One of the most frightening things about herpes is the number of serious complications you hear about. It is true that herpes can occasionally be very serious, but don't be overly concerned; just be cautious. The common cold can be serious as well. A cold can develop into pneumonia. A sore throat can sometimes produce kidney or heart damage in susceptible individuals. The point is that complications from herpes do occur, but they are rare.

Herpes can migrate from its resting place in the ganglia in the neck to the brain and spinal cord causing an inflammation called encephalitis (inflammation of the brain), or meningitis (inflammation of the membrane covering the brain and spinal cord). New drugs are available in many countries for treatment of these infections.[11]

Another rare happening is a herpes infection on the surface of the eye (the cornea). If untreated it can cause ulcers and eventually scarring of the cornea. However, there are several very effective treatments for herpes of the eye.[11] So if you feel that you may have an eye infection – especially if you have one close to the time you have a herpes attack – don't hesitate to check with your doctor.

Many researchers feel that genital herpes in women may increase their chances of cervical cancer.[5,12,13,14] The theory is that the herpes virus gets into the tissues of the cervix and alters the cells so that a cancerous change may occur. This is not a proven cause-and-effect relationship. But it is true that women who do develop cervical cancer are more likely to have had a prior history of genital herpes than women who have not. Just to be safe, if you know that you have herpes, be sure to get a Pap smear every six months to check for early signs of cervical cancer.

There is another possible link between herpes and cancer found in women. It is called squamous cell cancer and is found in the genital area called the vulva. Cancer of the vulva is most often found in women over forty, but recently it has been detected more frequently in younger women as well. Some specialists believe that this is because it is linked to herpes which is more common in younger women.[15] Although these genital cancers are common enough to make regular screening and examinations very worthwhile, there are many more people with genital herpes who never develop a cancer. Take the proper precautions and you won't have to worry. As with any disorder, early detection is very important. So, if you are a woman who knows she has genital herpes - be safe and get regular gynaecological examinations. Again, it is the common sense approach that eliminates much of the myth, misconception and danger of herpes.

The biggest concern for women with herpes involves pregnancy.[13] If you get your first active herpes infection during the first five months of your pregnancy you are three times more likely to have a spontaneous abortion. If you get your first herpes attack during the second half of your pregnancy, you have one chance in three of bearing a premature infant. So if you don't have herpes and are planning a pregnancy, be very careful. Exercise basic hygiene and make sure that you have no intimate contact with anyone with active herpes during your pregnancy.

If you are planning a pregnancy and already have herpes, you will want to take steps to prevent a recurrence during your pregnancy - especially during the time of delivery. If you have an active herpes infection at the actual time your baby is delivered, it is exceedingly risky for the newborn. About 40 per cent of infants who move through the birth canal (the vagina) will become infected by herpes if the mother has an active infection at the time. This is a very severe infection and is fatal to the newborn in about half of the cases. Symptoms will begin between twenty-four hours to one week after birth and may include irritability, poor appetite, skin vesicles, difficult breathing, vomiting and diarrhoea. But just as for adults with severe herpes infections in the brain and nervous system, infants can sometimes be treated successfully with intravenous medication. One study found that about one out of every 250 women with a known history of herpes had an active infection at the time of birth.[16] It is not going to happen to every mother who has a history of herpes by any means, but it is such a serious problem if it does happen that it is worth being careful.

If you do happen to be one of the unlucky ones who develop an infection at term, you may still be able to avoid an infection in your newborn infant if you cooperate with your doctor or midwife.[16,17,18] First, be sure they know if you have had herpes in the past. Even if you are not sure, tell them there is a possibility you may have it. Or if you have a partner with known herpes tell your obstetrician. They may be able to check you for incipient herpes infection by culturing fluid from your cervix every week or so during the last part of your pregnancy. This is a simple, painless and very accurate way to check for any possible infection. Then, if your culture is 'positive', that is, you are beginning to have herpes viruses showing up in the cervix, it suggests that you are developing an active infection. At this point, you can elect to have your child delivered by Caesarian section. In most cases, this will protect the newborn from infection. Cultures for herpes virus are not necessarily available in all hospitals, so be sure you discuss this with your obstetrician early in the pregnancy.

> Terry R. was about to get married. He knew he had herpes; his fiance Ann also knew he had herpes, but they didn't know what to do about it. When they came into the office for their examination, the subject came up. We told Ann that it was not inevitable that she would also get herpes. We instructed them both in the nature of herpes, nutrition, the use of lysine, and stress management. That was a year and a half ago. Ann has remained herpes-free and they are the proud parents of Edward, a happy and healthy two-month-old son.

Where Did I Get My Herpes?
Usually herpes is acquired from contact with someone who, knowingly or not, has herpes. A first herpes attack

will probably show up within a few days, though it can range from days to even months or years after exposure. Sometimes it is hard to track down the source. You may have acquired herpes from someone who wasn't even aware of being potentially infectious. And, you may have acquired it a long time ago. At that time you may not have known that the sores you had were herpes, or possibly have even forgotten the attack altogether. There are many reports of individuals who have recently experienced a first attack of genital herpes but have had no sexual contact at all for years.[19]

It is possible that herpes may spread without intimate contact with another individual. The chances are slim, but it may be possible to contract herpes from an inanimate object such as a piece of clothing, a face cloth, or a toilet seat.[20] Fairly recently, two US researchers demonstrated that the herpes virus can indeed live for several hours away from protection of the human body.[1] So a case of genital herpes should not and cannot be used as evidence of sexual activity. Yet some people are branded as sexually promiscuous because of a herpes diagnosis. This is patently unfair.

What Can I Do?
Fortunately there are steps you can take that actually reduce the risk of getting herpes or, if one has herpes, will help shorten or even avoid attacks altogether.

Just because you have herpes it doesn't mean you are completely helpless – you do have some control over whether or not you will get an active attack. Even the most conservative medical researcher will agree that herpes has a great deal to do with your general mental and physical health. It is well known that people who believe that they won't get a herpes attack have an advantage over people who worry about it. This is sometimes called the 'placebo effect'. In other words, many people who participate in studies to test the effects of different experimental treatments for herpes will get better, even though they were really only using a sugar pill (called a placebo). This is probably because they were less worried and less stressed – because they believed there is a chance the pill will work. And when one's stress level goes down, your immune system can function more effectively to fight off a recurrent infection. In addition, you can actively reduce your stress level by learning some simple stress management skills (see Chapter 5). You can accomplish a great deal toward improving your general health and strengthening your immune system with a good diet as well. And finally, you can use your diet to specifically help suppress the growth of the herpes virus by altering your dietary intake of the amino acids lysine and arginine. In the next few chapters you will learn more about these simple and extremely effective techniques for controlling your herpes and improving your general health as well.

> Martha F. was 77. She had been plagued by 'cold sores' for the last 50 years. She was embarrassed by them because they looked awful, and she always seemed to get them around family holidays. She was beginning to worry that her numerous nieces and nephews would think that she always had them. Besides, they hurt. When she came into the office she had a pretty bad case of them. Although the purpose of her visit was of a different nature, we asked her a little about her sores: how long they lasted, when she got them, and so on. We suggested some nutritional changes, lysine supplements, and stress management exercises. She was particularly careful the week before a family gathering. Martha is delighted. Her only recent outbreak was after a time when she simply forgot some of our tips and also spent a great deal of time in the sun. (She is quite a gardener.) We recommended she wear a broad-brimmed hat when gardening and not to forget our nutrition and stress reduction tips

3.
WHAT DOES NUTRITION HAVE TO DO WITH HERPES?

The question of nutrition is very simple. Good nutrition is vital to a body's health; poor nutrition can cause problems. When we are talking about herpes, the problem becomes very specific. If one's diet is full of 'empty calories' (foods that supply calories but no nutrition – such as refined flours, fats, sugars) your basic nutritional needs are not met. One of the things that happens is that you begin to lose your ability to resist infections – such as herpes – and you have more difficulty healing quickly and completely.

What do we mean when we say 'good nutrition'? Most experts agree that a good diet is high in fibre, vitamins and minerals and low in fat, refined (white) flours, salt, sugar, caffeine, alcohol and other drugs. Let's talk about what you can do to improve your overall nutrition. There are three simple things: (1) Eat more fresh fruit, vegetables and whole grains; (2) eat foods that are close to their natural state; and (3) eat often.

1. Eat more fresh fruit, vegetables and whole grains. In order to do this, limit your intake of fatty foods – red meat, butter, oils, cheese, cream, eggs. Cut down on foods that have been prepared with oils and sauces, too. For example, it is better to eat a slice of wholegrain bread – even if it does have some butter and jam on it – than to eat a doughnut. At least you are getting the nutrition and fibre that the whole grains contain. Of course, the less

butter and jam, the better, too. It's a good idea to watch your intake of fats and sugar.

In addition to containing a lot of fat, animal products have another intrinsic flaw: they have no fibre in them. Fibre is only found in plants. It is the 'indigestible' part of plants and is sometimes called bulk or roughage. Fibre is, in fact, 'indigestible', that is to say your body cannot break it down into small substances which can be absorbed into your blood stream. But fibre is still a very important part of your basic diet. Fibre promotes healthy digestion by stimulating normal movement of the intestine. It acts rather like a broom that helps to sweep waste matter out of your intestines. High-fibre diets have been credited with decreasing your risk of intestinal diseases (like cancer of the colon, constipation, colitis, diverticulitis and others). Fibre will also bind to cholesterol and remove it from your body, thus lowering the risk of heart disease, hardening of the arteries, and excessive weight gain. The more animal products you consume, the less fibre you have in your diet. Many nutritionists now recommend that you get about 60 per cent of your calories from high-fibre (plant) foods, about 15 to 25 per cent from fat, and only about 15 per cent from animal protein. (Most people in Western countries get 40-50 per cent of their calories from fats.)

2. Eat foods that are close to their natural state. These are called 'unprocessed foods'. A natural food like a fresh, crisp apple is much better than sweetened apple sauce or an apple pie. A steamed potato is much better for you than chips or potatoes *au gratin*. Fish is better than red meat, and grilled fish is better than fried fish. The general rule of thumb is that from a nutritional point of view, the less one does to food, the better it is. The worst example of the current trend in food processing madness is to take perfectly good wheat grains, which contain an enormous amount of vitamins, minerals and fibre in their covering

(bran) and core (germ), and then process them until the flour is white and basically nutrition-free and then throw all the good part of the wheat grain away. This unhealthy tradition comes from the old days when peasants ate brown or dark bread and royalty got all the fancy refined white stuff. Statistics show that peasants usually lived longer and healthier lives. So, when shopping, try to get foods as fresh as you can, and when cooking, do as little to them as possible. Fresh herbs and spices are a good place to start when wondering how to replace your butter and cream sauces.

3. Eat often. Contrary to the old adage of three square meals a day and no snacks in-between meals, it is, in fact, much better for your body to eat often – even if you are trying to lose weight. When you switch from a high fat and low fibre diet to one that is low in fat and high in fibre, your body will need a greater amount of food. The reason is this: high fat foods contain two or three times as many calories per serving as high fibre foods. Also, fats tend to stay in your intestinal tract (digestive system) longer. They move slowly and do not stimulate the digestive process. By contrast, high-fibre, low-fat foods stimulate digestion and move through the intestinal tract more easily and rapidly. It is important therefore to eat every few hours to keep from feeling hungry and from running out of steam. You will not gain weight. In fact, many people who switch over to this type of eating report that in spite of increased food consumption, they actually lose weight – not to mention feeling better and much more energetic. The key here, of course, is to eat the right *kinds* of foods often. High-fibre, low-fat foods are naturally low in calories and are more filling as well. But if your 'snacks' tend to go back to chips, dips, biscuits and such, you will be right back to the kind of eating you were doing before, only more of it. Here are some sample menus to give you a better idea about how to plan high-fibre low-fat meals:

For Breakfast, try:
  Whole fresh fruit (*not* juice, it has no fibre).
  Cooked wholegrain cereal (oatmeal, mixed grains, wheat, etc.) with fruit or skimmed (non-fat) milk.
  Wholegrain toast with small amounts of butter or fruit preserves or apple sauce (preferably prepared without sugar).
    [Try to avoid high-fat, low-fibre foods, like bacon, sausage, kippers, eggs, etc.]

For Lunch, try:
  Sandwiches (made with wholegrain bread and limited fat. For example, use chicken or tuna in water, instead of ham, beef or cheese; use mustard or yogurt instead of butter or mayonnaise; and use lots of vegetables like lettuce, tomatoes, mushrooms, onions, etc.)
  Grilled fish (don't spoil it by frying or adding fatty sauces or butter).
  Fresh vegetables in salads (with small amounts of fat in the dressing. Use vinegar and lemon with a *little* oil; or try buttermilk or plain yogurt flavoured with herbs).
  Steamed or boiled vegetables (potatoes, carrots, broccoli, marrow, etc.). Don't undo all their goodness and nutrition by overcooking or by loading them up with cheese, butter, sour cream or sauces.
  Soups. Again watch the fat content. Use small amounts of lean meats and trim the fat; load up with lots of vegetables and whole grains like barley and brown rice. Beans are good too – just don't add fat to them. You can make great creamed soups with powdered *non-fat* or *low-fat* milk.

Dinner Menus – The fish, vegetable and soup suggestions are fine for dinner as well. If you are accustomed to eating 'heavy' evening meals which emphasize meats, fish or fowl loaded with fatty sauces, try to change things around a bit; decrease the amount of meat and add a couple of extra low-fat vegetables; try using cooked whole grains as a main course occasionally – casseroles made with brown rice or millet, for example.

Snacks/Tea:
Fresh, whole fruit.
Crackers or wafers made with whole grains.
Biscuits using wholewheat flour, or other wholegrains such as oatmeal; and use limited amounts of sugar, oil/butter or eggs.

What About Vitamin and Mineral Supplements?

Generally speaking, our food today is lower in vitamins and minerals than ever before, even if one does eat a well-balanced diet. The soil it is grown in is likely to be more depleted of nutrients, and by the time it gets to the market and then on to the table, much nutrition is lost. For this reason a good general vitamin/mineral supplement may help you. Some health professionals – including doctors – still claim that vitamins and minerals are a waste of money. Commonly heard in medical schools around the world is: if you eat a well-balanced diet, you don't need vitamins. Possibly this is true in some *rare* instances in some *rare* parts of the world. However, apart from the fact that it is very hard to put together a well-balanced diet for everyone in the family these days, there is no guarantee that the foods you use will be full of vitamins and minerals. Even if one buys only foods that have not been processed, these foods have probably been in storage for several hours – if not days (or even months) – since their harvest, and have lost even more nutrients. Then once we get them home we tend to damage them even more; so by the time we bring the food to the table, no matter how 'well-balanced', they are in a sorry state indeed. Our bodies were designed to eat (and thrive on) lots of fresh fruits, vegetables and grains, but what we offer our bodies today is a far cry from the absolutely fresh, energy-packed foods our earliest ancestors used to enjoy. Taking a supplement which gives us assured levels of vitamins and minerals is a good idea.

In addition, most people have some special need for vitamin and mineral supplements. For example, if you are taking birth control pills, you need extra B and C vitamins. If you drink a great deal of coffee or tea, you may benefit from extra potassium. Smokers seem to use up their B vitamins more rapidly. Women over 50 need much more calcium and magnesium. All women who menstruate should take iron. People who exercise heavily may need extra zinc and magnesium. Many medications deplete vitamins in the body. And so on. A good overall supplement is often the answer.

Herpes victims are a special group who may also benefit from vitamin/mineral supplements.[21] There are several nutrients which have a demonstrated effect on the immune system. If you are deficient in any of them, you may be less capable of resisting a herpes infection.

- Deficiency of vitamins A, E and many of the B complex inhibits the ability to produce antibodies and white blood cells and may be responsible for increased incidence of infections in humans.

- Higher levels of vitamin C may improve immune responses.

- Several minerals are important in maintaining a healthy immune system as well: iron and zinc may be particularly important.

Specific nutrients may also help promote more rapid healing of the herpes sores. Specifically, vitamin C plus bioflavonoids (substances found with vitamin C in natural foods) have been conclusively demonstrated to double the healing rate of herpes sores around the mouth. In one experiment, healing occurred in about four days with 600 to 1000mg each of vitamin C and bioflavonoids taken daily. Healing took nearly ten days in the group given only a placebo (sugar pill).[6]

If you are interested in trying supplements, Table 1 describes a good basic programme. Be sure you always take vitamins with food, and try to buy brands which do not add sugar, food colouring, saccharin or other unnecessary, potentially harmful substances.

Note: If you have any medical problems or are taking any medications, check with your physician before you begin any vitamin/mineral programme to be sure that the vitamins or minerals will not interfere with your medications or create any problem for you. This is particularly important for anyone with kidney problems, intestinal/stomach problems, or if you have been put on a special diet for any reason.

Table 1: Daily Doses of Vitamins and Minerals

*   Vitamin A – 10,000 to 15,000 IU
*   Vitamin B complex[1] – 15 to 25mg
*# Vitamin C – 500 to 1000mg
\#   Bioflavonoids – 500 to 1000mg
     Vitamin D – 200 to 400 IU
*   Vitamin E – 200 IU
     Calcium – 500mg
     Magnesium – 250 to 500mg
*   Iron – 25mg
     Chromium – 100mcg
     Selenium 100mcg
     Manganese – 10mg
     Molebdenum – 20mg
*# Zinc – 30mg

*   Deficiency of these substances may depress your immune system and decrease ability to fight off infection.

\#   Substances shown to promote more rapid healing.

---

[1] B complex contains a 'balance' of different individual B vitamins. Look for one that has about 15 to 25mg each of B_1 to B_6, and smaller quantities (mcg = microgram) of B_{12} and folate.

4.
SUPPRESS HERPES – LYSINE AND ARGININE

Not only is what you eat important for good health, but for people with herpes 1 and herpes 2 what you eat can either increase or decrease chances of an attack. This is because your basic diet contains two particular food substances which either encourage the growth of the herpes virus or suppress it. These substances are called lysine (which deters herpes growth) and arginine (which promotes herpes growth). Lysine and arginine are two of the twenty-two amino acids found in varying combinations in the proteins contained in all living cells; but to date only lysine and arginine have been found to have any important effect on the growth of the herpes virus. Lysine and arginine are similar in their chemical structure and are rapidly transported in and out of cells, which use them as raw materials for many different chemical reactions. These two amino acids are found in most high-protein food. Meat, dairy products, eggs, nuts, grains, beans, seeds, fish, chicken – all contain various amounts of lysine and arginine. The trick is to increase your intake of lysine and decrease your intake of arginine.

The lysine-arginine hypothesis originated in 1952 when a group of US scientists discovered that lysine inhibited the growth of a herpes virus that causes brain infections in mice.[22] A few years later, other scientists who were studying viruses, found that lysine strongly inhibited growth of herpes virus in the laboratory, and that arginine strongly encouraged its growth. In fact, they found that the herpes virus could not grow at all without arginine.[23,24]

Let's take a closer look at how this actually works. The genetic material in the herpes virus (called DNA), which directs the growth of the virus, requires a great deal of arginine. If the virus cannot get arginine, it simply cannot make enough DNA to reproduce. Also, the genetic material in human cells contains more lysine (and relatively little arginine) so your cells don't need much arginine for their growth. And the more lysine, the better for your cells. In addition, as shown by the laboratory experiments, lysine somehow keeps the herpes virus from getting enough arginine. Lysine probably works by keeping your cells from absorbing the arginine that is present in your diet or which is manufactured by your body.

There are several ways lysine may keep arginine from entering your cells where the herpes virus is hibernating. As we mentioned, lysine and arginine are very similar in structure and are constantly being transported from intestine to bloodstream, from bloodstream into cells and out again. This movement in and out of cells is controlled by tiny proteins called carriers. These carriers bind to the lysine or arginine and literally carry it through the membrane which surrounds the cell. These tiny carriers are selective. A carrier which is designed to carry lysine or arginine will not carry anything else. It won't carry a sugar molecule or a fat molecule. They are too different in shape and size, and are easily recognized as *not* being lysine or arginine. However, lysine and arginine are so similar to each other that the carrier cannot tell them apart. Since we want more lysine in our cells than arginine, it is important to have more lysine floating around in the bloodstream, so it has a better chance of catching a ride on these tiny carriers into your cells. If there is enough lysine around, it can actually displace the arginine from the carriers. This type of displacement happens at several locations in your body – your intestine, kidneys (which filter the blood) and the cells which contain the herpes virus. Even if arginine does get into the cells harbouring the herpes virus, if enough lysine gets in as well, it tends to push the arginine back out. It may also increase the actual breakdown of arginine within the cells.[25]

Arginine can be made by your body's own cells, but the actual amount present in your body also depends on how much you absorb from your diet.[26,27] (This is similar to the situation with cholesterol. Your body makes some of its own cholesterol, but the amount which enters your body from your diet determines how much is present in your bloodstream.) So it's important to reduce the arginine in your diet.

Based on what we know about the way lysine and arginine behave in the laboratory experiments on herpes virus growth, and inside the human body, there is good reason to believe that controlling these amino acids in the diet may help stop herpes growth in people who already have herpes infections. In fact, there is good evidence that the lysine/arginine balance in the diet actually does make a difference for people with herpes infections. Here are three examples:

- Infants who have herpes often get herpes attacks when they are weaned from milk.[24] This is probably because milk diets increase lysine in the bloodstream, whereas cereal diets cause a decrease in lysine (and an increase in arginine).[27]

- One study describes a tribe of people who were severely malnourished. Although malnourished, they had no obvious viral infections. But when they were given more food they developed viral infections. This makes sense, when one realizes that even though they were starving, the food that they did eat was primarily milk (lysine rich). And we also know that starvation itself can produce low arginine levels and raise lysine levels. So these people did, in fact, have a very high lysine, very low arginine type of diet, such as it was. The extra food that was given to them was mostly cereal (high arginine)![27,28]

- People who eat large amounts of arginine-rich foods like nuts, peanut butter, chocolate and seeds, are more likely to get an outburst of herpes.[24] (These foods do not *cause* herpes. But if herpes already exists in the cells and is hibernating, these foods may stimulate the herpes virus to grow and produce an outbreak.)

Some Interesting Background Studies

Several scientific studies have shown that addition of lysine to the diet and strict avoidance of arginine-rich foods inhibit the recurrence of herpes attacks and shorten those which do occur.[25,29,30] On the other hand, many experts remain unconvinced. Some claim that the lysine-arginine theory is incorrect because they say that the amount of arginine in the body is constant. They speculate that because arginine is made by cells in the human body, the dietary intake of arginine cannot make any difference in the amount of arginine which is actually present in the cells which contain herpes. This is not an accurate statement. Studies have already been done which clearly show that arginine levels do change with diet.[26,27] Other critics of the theory cite studies which have failed to demonstrate any protective effect of lysine added to the diet.[31,32] However, when these studies are examined closely, one finds that the amount of lysine used is relatively low, the numbers of human subjects relatively small and that arginine was not reduced in the diet. In addition, human studies on lysine inhibition of herpes seem to ignore factors which affect how well or how poorly lysine is absorbed from the food in the intestine into the bloodstream. The amount of sugar and fat present is very important, as is the amount of protein present in the stomach. These substances can inhibit the absorption of lysine.[27] So, even though you may take lysine tablets, you may not absorb much if you take them with sugar (even fruit juice, for example), fat or protein. Taking lysine along with a regular meal of any kind, may, in fact, *prevent* its absorption.

It is also important to realize that in the laboratory it doesn't take much arginine to overcome the suppressive effect of lysine and start the herpes growing. In fact, the amount of arginine which stimulates herpes growth in the laboratory is about the same as the amount of arginine found in the human bloodstream after a high-arginine meal.[24,27] Arginine level must be kept low or it will overcome the effect of high lysine intake. It is not surprising that the scientific studies which try to measure the effect of lysine on recurrence of herpes are contradictory. It is, in fact, difficult to evaluate all these factors: lysine absorption, amounts in food, effects of fat, sugar, arginine intake and so forth. No wonder the scientists disagree among themselves. However, it is generally agreed that there is no known risk to adding lysine and restricting arginine intake. On the contrary, evidence seems to strongly point in the favour of lysine as an effective way to help control herpes. In 1982, the United States Federal Drug Administration reviewed lysine as a potential treatment for herpes virus. They concluded that there are no known side-effects from lysine in doses of up to three grams a day.[33] (They didn't test higher dosages.) Many people report using lysine in much greater quantities than this without experiencing side-effects.

In spite of the scientific confusion surrounding the lysine hypothesis, thousands of people have reported that they get significant relief from their recurrent herpes by using lysine.

Gwen H. had acquired herpes several years earlier. She had been to doctors who shook their collective head and told her there was no hope, no cure. So, for several years she had put up with attacks. Her outbreaks were very predictable. Just before her menses, like clockwork, she would feel the familiar tingle, which increased to soreness and the cycle went on from there. By the time she came into our office for a totally unrelated problem, she was resigned and depressed about her herpes. We put her on a three-fold programme straight away. Nutrition, lysine supplements with arginine restriction, and stress management. She was to pay special attention to the few days just before her period. It is now six months later and Gwen reports: 'I kept waiting for the familiar signs and couldn't believe that they were not coming. I waited. I anticipated. I really had little faith in this programme although I carried it out to the letter. When the attack never came, I chalked it up to a fluke and forgot about it. The second month I again waited. And waited. I began to think that the attack just might not come. It didn't. I was convinced. I have had one outbreak since then, but it was predictable because I was feeling a little smug and didn't follow the programme. I got less sleep than I needed and ate carelessly. If I pay attention, I feel that I have good control over the herpes. I may not be 'cured', but it's certainly the next best thing.

In a survey of over 4,000 herpes victims, the only therapies which had any lasting benefit were lysine therapy and stress management. In fact, over half the people who tried lysine reported a benefit.[34] This is more than you would expect if lysine had only a placebo effect. And even more amazing is the fact that most of these people had no instruction in the proper use of lysine. One can only imagine the rate of success had they all been aware of optimum usage.

A major national publication in the United States, *The Saturday Evening Post*, recently reviewed the lysine therapy and published a comprehensive series of articles on lysine treatment for herpes.[35] The editors also solicited reports of successful lysine use from its readers.[36] To use their words, 'Letters by the hundreds have been pouring in to the *Post* editorial offices in response to our July/August '82 *Post* article "Does L-lysine Stop Herpes?"' These success stories are very heartening. Many of the people who reported success with lysine/arginine therapy were chronic herpes sufferers who had tried a dozen or more remedies before success with lysine.

'In many cases, herpes sufferers report that they have conducted their own "placebo controlled" experiments by accident. For example, one patient said she started using lysine very enthusiastically but returned a few weeks later to the office very upset because she had experienced no improvement. She was still getting attacks every other week. In reviewing her diet and lysine regimen, we discovered that she had been taking a mixture of two types of lysine – the "d" and "l" forms. Only the "l" form is active in the human body (or in any living cells for that matter). The "d" form is a mirror image that simply doesn't work. So when she thought she was taking a 500mg tablet of l-lysine, she had actually been taking only 250mg of l-lysine (and 250mg of d-lysine). She went home with the correct form (pure l-lysine) and began to improve almost immediately – even though at this point she was quite sceptical. In this case, the "d" form of lysine was acting as a placebo (a sugar pill). And even though she strongly believed it would work, it didn't.'

Physicians who prescribe lysine receive this kind of report from their patients over and over again. Many people have found the lysine approach to be extremely effective. Some physicians feel that the success rate with l-lysine may be as high as 80 to 90 per cent.[25,29,35] That is, 80 to 90 per cent of people who use l-lysine correctly, and strictly avoid arginine-rich foods, experience an obvious reduction in either the frequency and/or the severity of their attacks.

Taking L-lysine Correctly

First, be sure you have obtained the correct form of lysine, namely l-lysine. It is available in health food stores that sell vitamins and minerals, is relatively inexpensive and does not require a prescription. Stick to a well-known brand because the chances are it will be cheaper and there may be less chance of getting a low quality product. Most l-lysine comes in 500mg tablets, although it is sometimes supplied in other sizes – like 330mg or 667mg tablets. It really doesn't matter – look for the best price. Take your lysine supplements at least three times a day (to help keep a high level in your bloodstream). Take your lysine on an empty stomach (the reverse of vitamin/minerals). This will help you absorb a greater amount of the lysine. If you do take it with a meal, avoid sugar and fat which may keep you from absorbing much of the l-lysine.[26,27]

The amount of l-lysine to use depends partly on whether or not you are trying to prevent an attack, or are treating an active attack. It also depends on the amount of arginine in the foods you eat. In addition, your general health, vitamin and mineral intake and stress level are important factors. Most people take 1000mg to 3000mg l-lysine a day to prevent attacks, and 3000mg to 8000mg a day for active herpes. (Remember to spread it out over the day and do *not* take it with meals.) No side-effects have been reported with these levels. There may, however, be some individuals who will notice some type of reaction, so do pay attention to how you feel after taking l-lysine (or any other type of concentrated food supplement) just as you would if you were taking a prescription drug.

The foods you eat are very important as well. Animal foods high in l-lysine (and low in arginine) include fish, milk, red meat and poultry. High l-lysine vegetables include soya beans and legumes (dried beans, butter beans, mung beans and beansprouts). Cheeses and eggs also have a relatively high l-lysine content, but they have so much fat that the lysine may not be that well absorbed. Also, the fat in milk, meat, fish and poultry could possibly interfere with absorption. So keep the fat minimal and use low or non-fat milk; don't fry fish or chicken, and trim your meat. High lysine foods (with low fat content) are listed in Table 2.

Table 2: High L-lysine Foods (Foods to Eat)

Portion	Food	mg Excess L-lysine
4 oz (115g)	fresh fish	+ 930
4 oz (115g)	shark	+ 880
4 oz (115g)	tinned fish	+ 810
4 oz (115g)	chicken	+ 740
4 oz (115g)	beef	+ 720
8 fl oz (230ml)	goat's milk	+ 520
8 fl oz (230ml)	cow's milk	+ 420
4 oz (115g)	lamb	+ 420
4 oz (115g)	mung beans	+ 410
4 oz (115g)	pork	+ 380
1 oz (30g)	cheese	+ 280
4 oz (115g)	beans, cooked	+ 270
4 oz (115g)	butter beans	+ 240
4 oz (115g)	cottage cheese, dry	+ 220
4 oz (115g)	mung bean sprouts	+ 210
1 tablet	yeast, brewer's	+ 190
4 oz (115g)	crustaceans (crab, etc.)	+ 170
4 oz (115g)	soyabeans, cooked	+ 130
8 fl oz (230ml)	milk, human	+ 100
3 oz (85g)	green beans	+ 30
3 oz (85g)	dates	+ 20
4 oz (115g)	spinach	+ 20
4 oz (115g)	asparagus	+ 20
1	peach	+ 20
4 oz (115g)	aubergine	+ 10

These foods contain more lysine than arginine. For example, a 4 oz (115g) serving of fish contains 930mg of excess l-lysine. This is about equal to two 500mg l-lysine tablets. (See Appendix for discussion of calculation method.)

Table 3: High L-arginine Foods (Foods to Avoid)

Portion	Food	mg L-lysine Deficiency
3 oz (85g)	hazelnuts	− 2250
3 oz (85g)	Brazil nuts	− 2110
3 oz (85g)	peanuts	− 2060
3 oz (85g)	walnuts	− 810
3 oz (85g)	almonds	− 710
3 oz (85g)	cocoa powder (chocolate)	− 650
2 tablespoonsful	peanut butter	− 510
3 oz (85g)	sesame seeds	− 450
3 oz (85g)	cashews	− 420
3 oz (85g)	carob powder	− 310
3 oz (85g)	coconut	− 290
3 oz (85g)	pistachio nuts	− 240
4 oz (115g)	buckwheat flour	− 230
4 oz (115g)	chickpeas	− 210
4 oz (115g)	brown rice	− 190
3 oz (85g)	pecans	− 180
4 oz (115g)	oatmeal, cooked	− 130
3 oz (85g)	sunflower seeds	− 120
4 oz (115g)	corn	− 80
2 slices	wholemeal bread	− 80
2 oz (55g)	wheat bran	− 80
4 oz (115g)	millet	− 60
1	yam	− 60
1	banana	− 30
2 slices	rye bread	− 30
2 oz (55g)	cabbage	− 30
4 oz (115g)	lentils	− 20
3 oz (85g)	grapes	− 20
3 oz (85g)	raisins	− 20
1	cucumber	− 20
1	tangerine	− 10

These foods contain more arginine than lysine, so there is a deficiency of lysine. For example, if you eat 3 oz (85g) of peanuts, you have a 2060mg lysine deficiency.

It is just as important to avoid foods which are rich in arginine (and low in lysine). The worst offenders are nuts and seeds of all kinds. Chocolate, or anything made from cocoa powder, is also a problem. Grains such as rice, wheat and oatmeal have a slight arginine excess. These foods are listed in Table 3. This list of foods is quite complete and comes from the 1970 edition of the Food and Agricultural Organization's book *Amino Acid Content of Foods*. Most other common foods either have no amino acids of any kind in them (low protein foods) like fruits and vegetables, or the amounts of lysine and arginine are pretty equally balanced.

Obviously, no one would recommend that you eat only fish and non-fat milk, and avoid all whole grains. However, we strongly recommend that herpes sufferers avoid nuts, seeds and chocolate, and use grains sparingly when actually having an attack. When you do eat animal protein, stick to fish and poultry, since red meat tends to be quite fatty, even though it does have excess l-lysine in it, and eat generous quantities of the 'neutral foods' like vegtables and fruits. Remember, arginine stimulates growth of herpes and it doesn't take much arginine in your diet to completely counteract the effects of lysine. So keep an eye on your lysine-arginine balance and don't hesitate to supplement with l-lysine tablets.

How long should you take l-lysine? A few days, weeks, years? That really depends on you. Some people who only get attacks once or twice a year do well just taking 3000 to 8000mg l-lysine when they feel an attack coming on. Others – usually individuals who are prone to frequent attacks (as many as two every month) – take lysine continually, increasing and decreasing the dose according to whether or not they feel an attack coming on. One man describes his situation by saying that he usually takes 1,500mg a day. But when he gets a cold, is short of sleep or goes off his diet at a party, he immediately increases his l-lysine intake. In this way, he has successfully managed his herpes for several years.

Some herpes victims find that they can discontinue l-lysine after several months, especially during periods when they are taking good care of themselves with lots of rest, a good low fat, low sugar and low arginine diet and attention to keeping stress levels low. The role of supplements, general health and stress levels are as important as a good lysine/arginine balance. The more complete your health programme, the greater your chances of controlling herpes. Each individual finds his or her own optimal programme by balancing good health, nutrition and stress management.

5.
STOP YOUR HERPES WITH STRESS MANAGEMENT

All herpes sufferers agree that it tends to recur when they are 'down', when they are feeling particularly stressed. Lack of sleep, overwork, excessive worry, grief, poor diet, smoking – all these factors may act as 'stressors' – things which put a strain on your body and/or mind. It really doesn't matter where your stressors come from – whether it is primarily mental and emotional stress, or physical stress. The result is the same. Your body, particularly your immune system, suffer. The herpes virus is an opportunist. Give it half a chance and it will begin to grow, reproduce, migrate out from its resting place in your nerve cells to the skin and start another attack of sores.

Your body's immune defences are constantly guarding you and attempting to keep the herpes virus in quiet hibernation so it can't cause a recurrence. Your immune system has several tools at its disposal – white blood cells, antibodies (complex proteins which bind to foreign invaders) and substances like interferon designed to inactivate invading viruses. While your immune system cannot completely eradicate the herpes virus (the way it can with some other kinds of viral or bacterial invaders), a healthy immune system can keep the virus quietly under control. But it must be in good condition. We have already discussed how nutrition is critical in maintaining a healthy immune system. And, of course, having good health habits of all kinds will help you resist a recurrent viral attack. There is one other important thing you can do for yourself – conscious stress reduction. This means learning how to consciously reduce the stress level in your body by reprogramming your nervous system, by teaching yourself to fully and completely relax.

This is the way it works. When you are under stress (when there are many stressors acting on you), your body reacts automatically and instantaneously with a stress response. This response is natural, instinctive and biologically designed to get you out of danger – to get you away from the stressor. This stress response is called the 'fight or flight' reaction. It prepares your body instantly for an emergency. First, the alarm system in your brain triggers the release of adrenalin from your adrenal glands. Within seconds, your muscles tighten (to help you fight or run), pupils dilate (to see better), blood pressure rises (to pump more blood to your muscles and brain), blood is shifted from skin to muscles, etc. Now, no one would want to lose this potentially lifesaving stress reaction. In fact, you couldn't stop it if you tried. It's entirely automatic. However, this stress reaction is very hard on your body, so it is designed to last for only a few minutes – just long enough to get you out of trouble. When the emergency is over, your body will naturally return to a more relaxed, normal condition by going through the 'relaxation response'. This will reverse all the emergency reactions – blood pressure goes down, muscles relax, blood returns to the skin. The difficulty is that in most of us our stress response is over-used so that we end up in a fight or flight condition most of the time, instead of just occasionally. We never really have a chance to get back to a normal, healthier, quieter state. We may even reach the point where our bodies forget the relaxation response.

This constant stress response will eventually catch up with you and your health begins to break down. It is like trying to keep an engine running at high speed – you can do it for a while, especially if you have regular maintenance checks and strictly limit the time the engine is working at high speed. But if the high speed abuse continues, it will inevitably break down.

Your body is no different. At some point it too will rebel. This may happen dramatically, such as a fatal heart attack. But for most people the breakdown is more subtle – getting colds all the time, finding that you are irritable and grumpy, or getting herpes attacks.

Herpes As a Sign of Stress

People with herpes often find that they react to stress with a herpes attack. In fact, this may be the very first sign of overstress in their lives. As the body begins to wear out, the immune system can't work as effectively and the ever-alert herpes virus takes the opportunity to begin growing again. The first time this link to stress is explained to new herpes victims, they may become very discouraged because they don't believe they can reduce the stress in their lives.

Some people even deliberately create stressful situations for themselves because they like the way they feel during a stress reaction. This isn't as crazy as it sounds. In the beginning, the stress reaction is very exciting, even pleasurable. It feels good to be extra alert with faster reflexes and greater strength. As a result, some people actually become addicted to the stress response – they become 'adrenalin addicts'. In fact, such individuals will even begin to believe that they can't function without a continuous stress response pouring adrenalin into their bodies. Unfortunately, the stress response that is over-used and abused will sooner or later become very harmful, even dangerous. Eventually it will seriously interfere with your ability to function by causing you to become ill – mentally and/or physically.

Actually, one can learn to function perfectly well without over-using the stress response for everyday existence. You can easily relearn your instinctive relaxation response. This will allow your body to repair itself and recover from the effects of stress and allow your immune system to function at peak strength to keep you in good health – and keep your herpes suppressed.

> Kate K. tells how the stress management part of her 'herpes programme' helped the rest of her life as well. 'I was getting very good at quieting myself during stressful situations – all the while telling myself that being calm would help keep my herpes away. Not only did it do this, and help me reduce the number of herpes outbreaks, but I noticed that by doing stress management exercises regularly I also felt better, was less impatient and it lowered my blood pressure as well.

Stress reduction isn't difficult to do. In the last decade scientists have developed effective ways to help individuals elicit the relaxation response and reduce ongoing stress levels. These reactions aren't unique to humans; in fact, much of the scientific work has been done on non-human animals such as mice.

Exactly how stressed are you? To some extent it depends on your individual lifestyle, how you cope and what you are already doing to reverse your stress response. But the number of external 'stressors' are important as well. Researchers have found that you can actually measure the amount of stress in your life by using a 'Stress Scale'. You may want to begin your stress reduction programme by obtaining your own stress score. (See Table 4, page 52.)

Relaxation techniques are basically simple. They are based on the principle of the mind-body connection – the biofeedback loop. The brain is linked to the body via special nerves called the 'autonomic nerves'. And the mind receives messages back from the body via sensory nerves. This forms a kind of loop. So if the brain is overactive (because of anxiety about stressors), it activates the body via the autonomic nerves; and when the body is tense and overactive, it communicates this to the brain via the sensory nerves. It really doesn't matter which comes first – physical tension or mental tension. The result is the same – a high stress level in mind and body. Relaxation techniques are designed to quiet mind and body simultanously. Because of the feedback loop, as the body becomes quieter, so does the mind and vice versa.

Here are three simple relaxation exercises you can use to reduce your stress level, two of them take only seconds and the third takes about fifteen minutes. The shorter ones can, and should, be integrated into your daily routine and be done several times throughout the day. Don't be discouraged if you don't notice results immediately. Your tensions probably took years to build up and won't disappear in a few days. However, after only a few weeks you will notice a definite improvement in your energy level and your general well-being.

Exercise One

This fifteen-minute exercise is one of the best for releasing tension. It actually burns up accumulated tension and teaches your body what deep relaxation feels like. (It is also good for toning muscles.) As you say each phrase, do it physically with your body, then let go and relax. Take in a deep breath as you tense, then let it out slowly as you relax. Make sure that you give yourself time to study and be aware of both the feelings of tension *and* relaxation.

1. 'I tense my scalp muscles.' (Now tense them as tight as as possible, to the point of trembling. Hold the tension, study the tension.)

2. 'Now I let go and relax.' (Exhale and relax. Give yourself time to study the feeling of relaxation.)

3. Repeat for:
Tighten eyes . . . Hold . . . Relax . . . Pause
Tighten jaw and ears . . . Hold . . . Relax . . . Pause

Hunch shoulders under ears... Hold... Relax... Pause
Tighten fists for hands and arms... Hold... Relax... Pause
Tense stomach... Hold... Relax... Pause
Tighten buttock muscles... Hold... Relax... Pause
Tense thighs... Hold... Relax... Pause
Tighten calves and feet... Hold... Relax... Pause

4. Follow with: 'I tense my entire body'.

5. Then, 'I let go and relax deeper.'

6. Complete by taking three slow deep breaths with long exhalations and a giant stretch.

How often? Whenever you feel tense (particularly after sitting or being still for a long period of time). At least once a day. Allow about fifteen minutes.

Exercise Two: The Breathing Check

Breathing is not simply a mechanism by which we take in enough air to keep us alive until the next breath. Breathing is fundamental to good health. All of our cells and organs need oxygen to keep functioning. Not only do we need oxygen to stay alive and healthy, but we need to get rid of carbon dioxide. The best way the cells have of getting rid of their waste carbon dioxide is to put it into the blood which is then purified by the action of the lungs.

The Breathing Check exercise will help you discover when you are breathing shallowly (upper chest) or deeply (from your abdomen). Complete deep breathing is one of the most effective ways to reduce tension, refresh yourself and generally help you feel better. Allow about one minute. Do it often during the day.

Exercise
Wherever you are – check your breathing. Ask yourself, 'Am I breathing quickly or slowly, shallowly or deeply?' Then, take a deep breath, hold it for a few seconds, and

then give a long exhalation. Make sure that you pull your abdomen fully in to push the air out. The exhalation is the most important part of this exercise. Your exhalation should take almost twice as long as your inhalation.

Try this. When you check your breathing, first breathe in and slowly count to 4 or 5. Then hold your breath for a count of 2. Then exhale fully, using your stomach to help push out the air and count slowly to 8 or 10.

Example:
 Breathe in . . . 1 . . . 2 . . . 3 . . . 4 . . . 5.
 Hold . . . 1 . . . 2.
 Breathe out . . . 1 . . . 2 . . . 3 . . . 4 . . . 5 . . . 6 . . . 7 . . . 8.

Do two or three of these at a time.

It may seem artificial at first, but as you practice, it will get easier. Soon you'll find that the Breathing Check will help you feel more relaxed. Your ordinary breathing during the day will gradually grow slower and more even.

How often? Do this as often as you can during the day. Practising in bed is a great idea also, especially if you have trouble sleeping.

Exercise Three: The Tension Check

Some tension is necessary. It holds you up. We need tense back muscles when we sit down to keep from falling over, and we need tension to move. But we do not want non-productive tension – the type of tension that serves no purpose – the toe-tapping, shoulder-hunching, or forehead-furrowing tension. The Tension Check will locate non-productive tension anywhere in your body and eliminate it. It can be done any place at any time.

Exercise:
Wherever you happen to be – standing, sitting, in a car, at home, or at work – take a moment to mentally go down your body. Move from head to toe, checking for non-

productive tension. Ask yourself, is my forehead furrowed, are my eyes tight, is my jaw clenched, how about my shoulders – are they hunched, are my fists clenched, is my chest tight? How about my stomach, is it tight?, is my bottom tense, what about my legs and feet? When you find tension that is not serving any purpose, let it go. There are two ways to do this. Either simply let it go as though you are letting go of a balloon on a string, or tense that muscle even more, hold the tension, and *then* let it go. The entire exercise takes only a minute or two and can be done almost anywhere. The important thing about this exercise is that you do it often. This exercise helps you let go of energy-draining tension, and gives you practice in the art of relaxing. In time, relaxation will become automatic.

How often? For optimum results do it often during the day. Allow at least one minute. If you practise these exercises each day you will notice a very significant reduction in your stress level after only a few weeks. You may sleep better, have less anxiety, make decisions more easily, and feel more optimistic. Physically, your energy level will increase, aches and pains may lessen and you will find yourself with fewer illnesses, including fewer herpes attacks.

It may be a nuisance to realize that you are more likely to get a recurrent herpes attack whenever you overstress yourself. But some herpes victims actually learn to use their herpes to their own advantage. It can become a 'stress indicator' for you by letting you know that you aren't taking care of yourself. And it is infinitely better than waiting for more dangerous signs of stress like serious mental or physical disease. So use your herpes, don't let it use you. Even though you won't ever really like the idea of having herpes, recognize that your herpes is a sign you are not taking good care of yourself. And then – do something about it!

The Evaluation Key

Not everyone is stressed by the same things. And not all stress is negative. A promotion creates stress, just as losing your job creates stress.

Constant stress can impair digestion, alter circulation and increase susceptibility to illness. Therefore, it is important to know how much stress you are living with and to learn how to control it.

The following test was developed by the authors to provide a means of estimating the amount of stress in your life.

Fill out the chart based upon experiences that have occurred in your life, or in the life of someone you love, during the past year. Then add up the point values as indicated. The scale at the end of the test will guide you in evaluating the score.

If your total score for the year is under 75, you probably will not have an adverse reaction.

A score of 75-125 indicates moderate stress, with some chance that you will feel the impact of that stress through physical symptoms. A score of 126-199 indicates severe stress, with a very real possibility that it will affect your health.

A score of 200 or more indicates very severe stress, with a high probability that your well-being could be threatened.

If you score high on the chart, it does not mean that you *will* become ill. You can take action to combat the effects of that stress by learning how to trigger the relaxation response. You can give yourself relaxation time every day so that your body will be able to recover from stress and regain its balance.

Table 4: The Evaluation Key

Experience	Point Value	Your Score
1. Death of child or spouse	100	
2. Death of close family member	75	
3. Marriage	75	
4. Divorce	75	
5. Separation from mate or spouse	75	
6. Personal injury or serious illness	75	
7. Prison term	75	
8. Reconciliation with mate or spouse	30	
9. Death of a close friend	30	
10. Serious illness in family	30	
11. Pregnancy	30	
12. Retirement	30	
13. Change to different occupation or career	30	
14. Change in financial status	30	
15. Loss of job	30	
16. Addition to family	30	
17. Change in number of arguments with mate or spouse	30	
18. Mortgage or loan over £25,000	30	
19. Significant personal achievement	30	
20. Foreclosure of mortgage or loan	30	
21. Mate or spouse starting or stopping work	30	
22. Change in responsibilities at work	30	
23. Starting or stopping school	30	
24. Change in living conditions	30	
25. Son or daughter leaving home	30	
26. Change in work hours or conditions	20	
27. Problems with employer	20	
28. Change in eating habits	20	
29. Change in social activities	20	

Experience	Point Value	Your Score
30. Change in residence	20	
31. Change in frequency of family gatherings	20	
32. Change in schools	20	
33. Change in sleeping habits	20	
34. Christmas	20	
35. Holiday	20	
36. Minor violations of the law	20	
37. Concern about loved ones	10	
38. Concern about personal finances	10	
39. Unhappiness about weight or physical fitness	10	
40. Too many things to do/not enough time	10	
41. Not enough to do/too much time	10	
42. Beginning to misplace or lose things	10	
43. Feeling lonely/being alone	10	
44. Difficulty managing time	10	
45. Concern about sex	10	
46. Concern about your future	10	
47. Car maintenance/transportation problems	10	
48. Concern about personal health	10	

YOUR TOTAL

6.
WHEN YOU GET AN ATTACK

If you have reason to believe that you may be getting a herpes attack for the first time, go to a clinic or physician as soon as the first sores appear so that you can establish whether or not you actually have herpes. Sores are in the genital area are not necessarily herpes. There are several other conditions which can look like herpes: fungal infections, syphilis sores, boils, abrasions, allergic reactions and other conditions can all mimic herpes. It is important to be sure. Another reason to check with a health professional is to be sure that you don't have a second infection in addition to herpes. If your herpes is sexually transmitted, you may have picked up gonorrhoea, trichomonas, syphilis, chlamydia, or some other infection as well. Don't be shy and don't delay. All these conditions can be detected fairly easily and can be treated and cured very quickly. If you suspect that your herpes is not from sexual contact, see your physician or clinic anyway. It may still be confused with another condition which has a simple and effective treatment. Cold sores around the mouth, for example, can be confused with impetigo, a bacterial infection which is usually treated with penicillin.

Once you know that you definitely have herpes, treat your attack just as you would any other infection or illness – take care of yourself. Reduce your work schedule as much as possible, so you can get more rest. Get on a better diet right away. Eliminate any junk food from your diet; that includes sugar, refined flours, artificial ingredients and preservatives. Now is the time to make sure you are not getting any arginine-rich foods (review the list on page 40). Then increase your l-lysine intake with foods and supplements. Begin a good basic vitamin supplement programme (see Table 1), and make sure that you immediately incorporate some stress reduction exercises into your day.

All these measures are designed to help stimulate your immune sytem, which in turn will help to suppress growth of the herpes virus, and allow healing to occur as rapidly as possible. Many people who have had frequent herpes attacks over the years report good success with this three-fold approach. By increasing their lysine and decreasing their arginine, by supplementing with vitamins and by engaging in some type of stress reduction programme, they are often able to stop an attack in its tracks, before it develops into a full-fledged case.

> Jean always knows when she is about to get an attack of genital herpes because she notices a definite tingling and irritation about twenty-four hours before the sores actually appear. Now, as soon as Jean notices the tingling, she immediately steps up her self-care programme. 'I look at the lysine/arginine list and cut out all foods that are listed under arginine and eat as much fish and dairy products (low-fat) as is sensible. Then I take about four 500mg l-lysine tablets three times a day and vitamin C as well. Then – and I think this is very important for me – I make sure to get at least eight hours sleep at night. By the end of the second day of this routine, I notice the tingling is gone and the sores which should have developed – haven't. I keep on this routine for a day or two more, then go back to my old schedule, except I pay a little more attention to lysine, arginine and stress.'

Another thing to consider when you get an attack is your attitude. Don't be too hard on yourself for 'letting it happen'. Even though you may have worked out the best possible prevention plan for you, there are times when you may not be able to follow it, and an outbreak of herpes will occur. Don't add to the discomfort of the attack by being too hard on yourself or by being discouraged and feeling as though you have made no progress whatsoever. The thing to do at this point is to get back to your programme and help heal the attack as rapidly as possible. Try to avoid a negative attitude which puts additional stress on your nervous system and may slow the healing process. Now is the time your body can best benefit from a more positive view of the situation. You can take the opportunity to see what you had been doing right and what went wrong so you can keep it from happening again. Either way, it is very important (just as important as caring for your physical self) to maintain your mental health so your immune system can get back on the right track.

Medications
Several kinds of medications are becoming available which are specifically designed to treat herpes. Many are potent, may have side-effects, and not all are effective for all forms of herpes. They may be useful to you if used selectively, properly and under careful medical supervision.

Acyclovir is a well-tested medication which is becoming widely available for treatment of certain kinds of herpes infections. Acyclovir works by preventing the herpes virus from manufacturing more genetic material (DNA) while inside your cells. As a result, it may keep certain recurrent infections under control or speed healing of sores.[11,37,38] Acyclovir comes in three forms: ointment for the skin, pills and as an intravenous medication.

1. *Ointment:* Acyclovir ointment can be helpful for genital herpes *if it is your first attack, and if you start using it right away (within 24 hours or less)*. Under these circumstances, sores

may be less painful and will heal more quickly. The ointment doesn't do much for recurrent attacks. It does not have any effect on herpes type 1 around the mouth.

2. *Pills:* Acyclovir pills are available in some parts of the world, and may be more effective than the ointment. They may be used for treating active attacks and may even have some ability to prevent recurrences in some cases. They can be effective on recurrent cases as well as first attacks.

3. *Intravenous Acyclovir:* This is used in a hospital setting for people who are susceptible to severe genital herpes attacks because their immune systems are suppressed. Intravenous Acyclovir is also quite effective for treatment of herpes zoster (shingles) in people with normal or suppressed immune systems. It can decrease pain and swelling and speed healing.[39]

Since Acyclovir is a prescription medication and relatively new on the scene, check with your doctor to get the latest information if you think it will be helpful for you. It seems safe, and serious side-effects have not been apparent. However, some herpes virus infections have already shown 'resistance' to Acyclovir.[40] This means that they have somehow changed their DNA duplication process to overcome the suppressive effect of Acyclovir. If this kind of resistance becomes common, then Acyclovir will become less effecive and the herpes virus will become even harder to treat.

Vidarabine is another antiviral medication which can be an effective treatment for the serious herpes simplex infections of newborns. It may also help in treatment of the brain infections (herpes encephalitis), herpes infection of the eye and in herpes zoster (shingles). However, it is not helpful for the most common forms of herpes simplex 1 and 2 which affect the lips and genitals. There have also been some side effects reported, such as nausea, vomiting, diarrhoea, tremours, seizures.[11]

Trifluorothymidine and **Idoxuridine** are also used for the treatment of herpes eye infections.[11]

Isoprinosine is a promising oral medication which may be effective against several kinds of herpes.[41,42,43] It seems to be relatively non-toxic. Isoprinosine works by stimulating the immune system, rather than by suppressing viral growth. It is currently undergoing extensive testing but is not available in Britain yet.

Herpes research is active throughout the world, and more and more medications will become available in the next decade. Most of them are designed as treatment for attacks, rather than actually being a permanent cure. Examples are interferon (an antiviral protein),[11] phosphonoformate (being developed in Sweden, to treat herpes skin infections), and bromovinyldeoxyuridine (BVDU).[11,44,45]

There have also been several attempts to develop an effective vaccine for herpes. A vaccine is a substance which stimulates the immune system against a specific type of disease. Then, when you are exposed to a particular virus, your immune system will keep it from infecting your body, or it will help your immune system suppress recurrent attacks.

Vaccines which have been tried, but do not work for herpes, include smallpox vaccine and BCG vaccine (developed to prevent tuberculosis). These vaccines have definite side-effects and should not be used for herpes.

Lupidon H and Lupidon G are anti-herpes vaccines which have been developed and manufactured in Germany for type 1 and type 2 herpes. The vaccines are most effective for preventing recurrences in patients with both type 1 and type 2 herpes. Unfortunately, the treatment is rather lengthy and complex. The French have produced a similar vaccine called Lepine. Both German and French vaccines have been criticized because of the possibility that they could (theoretically) enhance tumour growth. Better vaccines may be developed in the next few years.[5,46,47]

The biggest danger with the push to develop better medications to treat herpes is that it distracts us from remembering that the most important aspect of treatment of herpes is how well we take care of ourselves. Medications are important, and can even be lifesaving, but they are no substitute for an active and consistent self-care programme which keeps your immune system healthy, suppresses viral growth and promotes rapid healing.

Caring For Herpes Sores

When you do experience an active herpes attack, you will want to take care of the pain, swelling and sores.

Pain and swelling may be relieved by careful application of ice to the affected area early in the attack.[48,49] Take a few ice cubes, wrap them in a paper towel and place them directly on the herpes sore, on and off for 1 to 2 hours. This should help the swelling and numb the painful area. Do this as often as you feel it is helping you. Another totally different approach (to show the individuality of herpes sufferers) is to apply warm compresses or a hot water bottle to the area. Whichever approach you use, keep in mind that this is sensitive skin and be careful not to 'freeze' or 'burn' the area.

You may also speed healing of sores by applying a solution of zinc sulphate (ask your pharmacist or physician for .025% to .05% zinc sulphate in water). Apply the solution to a sterile gauze pad and hold the moist pad on the sores for about ten minutes.[50,51]

Some people also report rapid healing and pain relief from the application of aloe gel (juice from the aloe plant). They apply the gel to the sores three to four times a day. (Aloe does promote skin healing and is used in hospitals to treat serious burns.)

Herpes sores, like any skin sore, can become infected by bacteria which are found on the skin. So it is a good idea to keep the area clean and dry in between treatments. In the case of genital herpes, it is advisable to wear 100 per cent cotton garments next to the skin.

One way to reduce chances of a bacterial infection is to use a 10 per cent povidone-iodine solution on the sores twice a day. (This treatment may also speed healing of herpes sores.[52,53]) Apply the solution with a sterile cotton-tipped applicator or sterile gauze pad. In addition, you may want to apply the solution to the sores *after* the ice or zinc sulphate treatment. (CAUTION: some people are allergic to medications containing iodine. Don't use this or any medication if you experience discomfort, rash, burning, or redness after its use.) Also, it is a good idea not to touch the sores directly when treating the affected area. Use a sterile pad, cotton-tipped applicators, etc. If you do touch the sores directly, be sure to wash your hands as soon as possible.

Women with genital herpes may experience excessive vaginal secretions during a herpes attack. This may be part of the body's response to the herpes, or may signal the presence of a second infection caused by yeast, bacteria or some other micro-organism. If the discharge doesn't clear up by the time the herpes sores have disappeared, consult your medical specialist for assistance in diagnosis and treatment.

During an attack of genital herpes, it is a good idea to wear loose clothing and pure cotton underwear. Herpes is uncomfortable enough without adding the discomfort of binding clothing. Don't use lotions, cream or powders on the affected areas. This may actually irritate the area, cause moisture retention and increase the possibility of further infection. If you have herpes around the mouth or lips, avoid facial makeup, lotions and lipsticks.

Normal bathing is probably best accomplished by showering during the time of a herpes outbreak. Rinse the area around the sores with plain warm water and avoid using a facecloth or any harsh soaps that might irritate the area. Remember to gently pat the area dry with a clean pad. Don't rub the sores or use the pad on other areas of the skin.

There is no doubt about the fact that herpes is painful. However, these simple methods will give you considerable help in minimizing the discomfort of an active herpes attack.

7.
PREVENTION AND PROTECTION

Herpes has been called an epidemic – and with good reason. It is extremely common, contagious, can be painful, is occasionally dangerous and, as yet, it is uncurable. But it is not necessary to feel helpless or hopeless. If you don't have herpes, you can take simple measures to decrease your chances of contracting it. If you do have herpes, you can learn to control and even prevent attacks. If you do experience active herpes attacks, you can still protect yourself from any complications and can avoid passing it on to friends and family. You are not helpless. In this chapter we will describe some simple ways to protect yourself and your loved ones from the fear of herpes – whether or not you have the disease.

Remember, herpes is spread by contact. This happens most easily with skin-to-skin contact – especially moist skin. So mouth, lips, genital tissues, rectal tissues and eyes are especially vulnerable. It is also possible (but not very likely) to pick up the herpes virus from inanimate surfaces, such as toilet seats or moist cloth. 'Auto-innoculation' may occur as well. This is when individuals with an active herpes sore accidentally touch the sore and then transport the virus to another part of their body – such as their eyes.

If you already have herpes, you can keep from spreading it to other parts of your body by observing a few common sense rules. Just remember that the virus abounds in the fluid produced by herpes sores, and avoid touching or spreading the fluid. When treating the sores, use a cotton-tipped applicator or clean pad; if you do touch the sores, wash your hands as soon as possible to keep from re-infecting yourself. Be particularly careful not to touch your eyes. When bathing, try not to rub the sores and avoid the use of harsh ointments or soaps on the affected area. Stay out of direct sunlight, especially for herpes type 1 around the mouth. Continue these precautions until the sores are completely healed.

If you already have herpes, you can avoid passing it on to someone else. Use the following guidelines: when you have active sores, avoid any direct contact between your sores and another person's skin. Don't share facecloths, towels, eating utensils or anything that may have come in contact with your sores. To play it safe, avoid touching and intimate contact if you even suspect you are coming down with an attack, and wait two or three days after the sores are completely healed. (It is possible to pass on the herpes virus just before and immediately after, as well as during an attack.) If you have genital herpes, you may want to play it extra safe by using condoms whenever you have sexual intercourse, even though neither partner has active sores. A recent study provides evidence that the herpes virus cannot move through condoms.[54] In any event, *never* have sex when the sores are present. Even if you use condoms, it is too risky. There is also some new evidence that chemical spermicides contained in contraceptive sponges, foams, jellies and suppositories may help prevent the herpes virus from being passed on between sexual partners.[55]

How Will I Know If Someone Else Has It?
If a person has herpes simplex around the mouth, the situation is pretty obvious. Usually the sore is clearly visible. Most people readily talk about it. It is usually easy to say that one has a 'cold sore'. There is not much of a

social stigma attached to having 'cold sores'.

But what about genital herpes? You probably won't know if somebody has herpes unless you ask directly, or unless your partner volunteers the information. And in some cases, one may not even realize that one has it. Here is where it is important for you to be knowledgeable and willing to communicate honestly with one another.

Some people are so upset by having genital herpes that they decide to become celibate rather than take the chance of passing it on. Very often, however, the real problem is their inability to talk about it. It is a very personal and difficult subject, but it can be done.

After a little practice, you will find that you can initiate a conversation about herpes (and about sexual health in general). One good way to begin is by making an 'I' statement. That is, start talking about yourself.

> I just wanted to let you know that I don't have any infections that I could pass on to you. I have had herpes attacks in the past, but I haven't had one for six months, and I can usually tell ahead of time before I get one.

This approach, while demanding nerve, is worth it. Your partner is likely to feel more trusting towards you and very often it will encourage him or her to make a statement about his or her own sexual health. Other approaches are:

> I just wanted to let you know that as far as I know I don't have any kind of infection I could pass on to you. But I know how common infections are, so I guess I've been lucky. Do you have any sign of infection like herpes that *we* should be careful about?

or

> I was just reading this medical article about how using

condoms and spermicides for birth control may also help protect against herpes. But as far as I know, I don't have herpes. Do you know whether or not you have?

It isn't easy to bring the subject up, but do it. For your sake and your partner's sake. You may be embarrassed, and may even find that some people will refuse to talk about it, or will even want to end the relationship. But it is well worth the risk. Honesty is the best way to begin a relationship. Would you want to be with someone who would lie to you?

Getting Some Help
If you are having a lot of trouble coping with herpes, don't be surprised or discouraged. Many people go through a period of emotional shock when they first discover they (or their partner) have acquired herpes. You may feel angry as well. Don't worry. You have every right to feel angry. In most cases, you can't just ignore it and wait for it to go away. It forces you to make some changes in your life, whether you like it or not. It is hard not to feel contaminated and persecuted at first.

If you have a friend with herpes, you might get together to exchange information and support. It always helps to share fears and find out how another person copes with a problem. You might also organize a small support group. Pass the word among friends and you may be surprised at how many people are affected by herpes and how easy it is to get a group together for education and emotional support.

—Ask your local family planning clinic or doctor if they can direct you to any groups or organizations which assist herpes victims. Such groups are becoming very common.

—You may want some private counselling as well. Again, contact a medical specialist in family planning or a therapist who specializes in sexual problems. (Be sure the person you select has experience with herpes sufferers and knows about the disease. You need someone who is really knowledgeable.) Talking to an experienced health professional can really help you enormously.

Treat yourself to some help and comfort. Don't punish yourself further by trying to go it alone.

Keeping Track

One of the things that we have noticed over the years when dealing with our herpes patients is that each person soon develops a specific pattern to their outbreaks. One person will get an attack whenever he is short of sleep; another will always break out right before her period. Each individual is most susceptible to herpes in certain situations. Keeping a herpes diary really helps you identify your pattern. Keep this chart for the next four to six herpes attacks and see if you can find your own area of vulnerability. Once you figure this out, you can plan effectively to prevent future attacks.

Date of Attack	Diet	Mental Stresses	Arginine-Rich Foods	Sleep	Other

Living with Herpes

Herpes is coming out of the closet. It is no secret anymore. When millions of people have a disease, it doesn't make sense to refuse to talk about it or pretend it isn't there. Having herpes is not a sign of promiscuity or weakness or moral turpitude. You will learn to coexist with your herpes virus.

If you do acquire a herpes infection, you will quickly learn how to control it – to keep your herpes virus quiet and inactive. At worst, your herpes may become active on occasion and you may view it as a nuisance. At best, you can learn to use your herpes virus to your advantage – as a stimulus to improve your overall health, which not only keeps the virus quiet, but will improve the quality of your life. So don't delay any longer. Take control now.

8.
ANOTHER APPROACH TO HERPES

It is vitally important when dealing with a chronic and pervasive problem such as herpes to explore every avenue to assist in finding a way to alleviate or control the problem. We have talked about the life of the herpes virus, what type of virus it is, how it gets about, how it thrives, and things to do that help subdue it. We have mentioned drugs, vitamins, lysine and nutrition. There is also a discussion of prevention and protection and how to limit attacks with stress reduction. All of this information is current and scientifically sound. It comes from our clinical experience as well as studies done by other researchers and physicians. The general consensus seems to be that if one takes care of oneself, eats lysine-rich foods, avoids arginine-rich foods, supplements with lysine and practises stress management, that one can pretty much control and minimize herpes outbreaks. Our experience substantiates this. There is, however, another aspect to dealing with herpes that is not mentioned as often – one which is equally important. This approach is not a scientific one, and therefore, not possible to prove, but it is one which can have a major effect on you and your body and your herpes. This approach is one that, with a little bit of practice, becomes not only effective in dealing with herpes, but plays an important part in your overall health and feeling of well-being. We are referring to the role our thoughts and feelings play in influencing our health – specifically our immune system.

ANOTHER APPROACH TO HERPES

The influence of our minds over our bodies is often overlooked when discussing ways to prevent the recurrence of herpes. Learning to tap the resources of our minds is as important in helping prevent an outbreak of herpes as good nutrition or stress reduction. Negative feelings about having an 'incurable disease' can be physically debilitating. Alternatively, adopting a positive attitude with regard to herpes not only can reduce the number of attacks you may have, but it can also promote rapid healing of the attacks you do get. Psychological factors are as important as physical factors with herpes control. The mind's power over the body is best demonstrated by the 'placebo effect'. Technically, a placebo is a 'sugar pill' – something which a patient believes will help but which really has no curative properties. The placebo effect has been documented countless times. Some studies involve people with herpes who volunteer to help test a new herpes drug. Often these people show improvement, even though they are given a placebo instead of the actual drug being tested. Taking advantage of this type of power is very important to herpes sufferers.

Dana G. was having recurrent herpes attacks every month. She tried everything that she had ever heard of to help her get over the attacks sooner or to lengthen the time between attacks. She did everything she could except allow herself to think of the possibility of not getting attacks at all. She tried lysine, but some people told her that it wouldn't really work, and it didn't. She tried creams and ointments, but even before she tried them she 'knew' that they were only superficial and would have no real effect on her attacks or their frequency. They didn't. She tried listening to relaxation tapes for stress management but didn't see how that could affect a virus in her body. It didn't. No matter what was suggested, Dana knew ahead of time it wouldn't work. Not because she was a naturally negative person, but because Dana had heard over and over again that herpes was 'incurable', and that there was 'nothing to be done'. Dana had given herself no options. By the time she came to us (for a totally unrelated problem), she was in a state of total resignation about her herpes. She was going to get an attack of herpes once a month, and that was that. We persuaded Dana to join our herpes support group. The group was composed of about a dozen people whose experiences with herpes had started in much the same way, and who, over the months, had managed to turn their thinking around to gain some control over herpes. Dana made her views about herpes known right away. Many of the other members of the group nodded and said that they knew how she felt. They had felt the same way. To be told by every doctor you see that there's nothing to be done and to read all the negative things about herpes that the press puts out, it is hard to have any optimistic feelings about herpes. One of the members of the group, Jack, told Dana that he had felt exactly the same way but that he had had the good fortune to meet Sally, who brought him to a support group meeting. Since joining, he had, over the months, been able to make some changes in the way he viewed herpes and himself. 'With me, a lot of it was self-image,' he said. 'I somehow felt that since I had caught this "shameful disease", I must not be a very good person, and I probably deserved it. All in all, I got into a very dejected state. Then I met Sally who brought me to this group and little by little I've started to feel more positive and even hopeful. In the group I've heard some success stories about ways to handle herpes. So, when I try them, like lysine or relaxing, I actually think that maybe they'll work, and they're beginning to!'

Dana, needless to say, was not convinced, but just being a part of the group was such good support for her that she gradually began to let go of some of her preconceived notions about the hopelessness of the situation. Learning that other people had the same problem was really helpful to her. And hearing what each person had done to relieve or prevent attacks gave her just enough confidence to try some approaches on her own.

First of all, she learned not to think of herpes as incurable. There is nothing more defeating than thinking that 'there is nothing to be done about it.' There are, in fact, many things to be done about herpes. In fact, our bodies are constantly curing herpes. Each time we have an outbreak, what happens? Our bodies cure themselves. And all the time that we *aren't* having an attack our body is suppressing the herpes infection. Language is a subtle and pervasive thing. Because we use language automatically and continuously, it can influence us more than we would suspect. So, for starters, NEVER refer to herpes as incurable or hopeless. This contributes to feelings of helplessness, isolation and despair.

Omit words in your vocabulary such as 'incurable', 'helpless', 'hopeless'. Begin to focus on the steps you can take to prevent an attack as positive things in your life. You have an entire array of inner resources that can help you to maintain your health. Some of the most famous work in this area has been done by Carl Simonton, M.D. As a part of his therapy for cancer patients, Dr Simonton has his patients spend some time each day relaxing and then 'visualizing' (forming mental images of) their bodies healing and their tumours shrinking. Simonton found that it doesn't matter exactly what the visualization is as long as it showed the tumour getting smaller and smaller. One patient might imagine the tumour looked like a hill being levelled by bulldozers; another would see the tumour as a huge snowball being melted by a warm rain; and another described visualizing a mass of enormous purple cancer cells being steadily demolished by an army of white knights with lasers. His results have been outstanding. Patients have been able to shrink their tumours from the size of a grapefruit to the size of a bird seed, with some cases disappearing altogether. What is the secret? Simply accepting the possibility that, given the proper environment and direction (relaxation and visualization), our bodies will heal themselves.

The procedure with herpes is no different. Spend some time each day to relax and then, after you feel relaxed, visualize either the herpes quickly subsiding (in the case where one has an active attack) or simply visualize a healthy body with energy and an active immune system (in the case where prevention is the goal). Use any image you like – white blood cells capturing or engulfing the herpes virus or a bolt of light disintegrating the virus. Use your imagination! The only prerequisite is a willingness to believe that this is possible. Since it has been documented as possible, you might as well let yourself accept the possibility that it will work for you, too.

Give yourself some time to put this type of programme into effect. Allot about twenty to thirty minutes each day to practise. Begin each practice session by relaxing. Either listen to a relaxation tape, visualize your muscles relaxing, or see yourself in a quiet environment (see Chapter 5 for more information on relaxation). Allow about ten to fifteen minutes for this part of the exercise. Then allow another ten minutes for the actual visualization. This procedure has been used not only for physical healing and prevention, but to help with changing your behaviour as well. During the visualization phase, mental suggestions can be added – such as I am growing more confident in my job, or I can see myself as a non-smoker, etc. This is a truly powerful tool for self-change, and if you give yourself the opportunity it can work for you.

After you have become relaxed, then begin your imaging. Be as specific in your image as you can be. See your immune system growing strong and able to do away with viruses. Begin to translate your image into an actual feeling – one of being healthy. After you have spent some minutes on this, allow yourself to relax even further or even drift off to sleep. This has the power to help fix the image in your subconscious. Be sure that you allow a month or two for the results of this process to begin to become apparent.

Don't neglect to preface your imaging with relaxing. The period of relaxation is important, in so far as it is the time when you make the transition from your conscious mind (the part of your mind that you work with most of the day) to your subconscious (the part of your mind that has a much more direct connection with your body and its immune system). That is the reason that visualization or imaging is such a powerful tool.

Certainly we are more than a body and even though we are dealing with something as obviously 'physical' as a herpes virus, it affects not only our physical state, but our mental state as well – our whole being. And if we use our whole being to combat it, we cannot help but win!

There is in fact much we can do about herpes and when we take care of ourselves by eating well and dealing with our stresses, we begin to feel that we have control over our herpes. We aren't victims and our feelings of helplessness disappear.

You might even acknowledge that it is a good idea that you make some changes in your life anyway – dealing with stress, getting more sleep, eating better, giving up chocolate. Perhaps you should have done some of these things long ago. One of the group members, Jim, was not so sure about the last point. Jim had a thing about fudge. Fudge represented to Jim all the good things in life. He'd eat fudge when he was depressed, he'd eat fudge when he was happy. When he got a good result in an exam, he'd eat fudge to celebrate. When he got a bad result, he'd have some fudge to console himself. Not that he ate fudge constantly. But he did eat it often.

> It sounds ridiculous, I know,' says Jim, 'but when it became clear to me that it was either fudge and herpes or no fudge and no herpes, I actually had to stop and consider. Like that old joke, where the burglar comes up to a miser and says, 'Your money or your life.' The miser pauses and the burglar says, 'Well?' And the miser says, 'I'm thinking, I'm thinking".

So I did stop and think about it, then I realized, chocolate *and* walnuts, that was really asking for trouble. So I gave up fudge (except on *very* rare occasions) and watch my intake of other high-arginine foods. I hate to sound smug about this, but my attacks are so few and far between that I almost consider myself an ex-herpes sufferer.

Jim's story is not unique. There are many success stories about people who learn to control their outbreaks; many by just following the book with regard to diet and stress reduction; others have incorporated a definite programme of 'positive thinking', some simply changed their eating and sleeping patterns. What works for Jim or Sally or anyone else may not work for you. But *there will be something that will work for you*. One thing, or combination of things, will help *you* gain control over a problem you once considered hopeless. And no matter what you choose, remember that your changes are positive and beneficial to your whole life; view yourself as a good person – not one who needs to be punished. Herpes gives you an opportunity to deal with unresolved stresses. It lets you take better care of yourself. All of this will help you to view herpes in a more positive light. Right away you have begun to have more control.

9.
INTERVIEWS

We have found that support groups are very important when dealing with a problem such as herpes. Knowing that other people are in the same boat and finding out how they cope often takes away some of the loneliness and fear. People who have had herpes for a long time, as well as those who have just discovered that they have it, profit from learning about the feelings and experiences of others. This chapter is meant to provide you with that kind of support. We have interviewed eight people with herpes and asked them several questions. When did you get herpes? Has having herpes changed your life? If so, how? Have you told anyone you have herpes? If so, how have people reacted? What did you do when you first found out you had herpes? How do you handle your outbreaks? Not everyone answered all of these questions, but we think that the information here will be helpful to anyone with questions about herpes.

Interview 1
Karen G., 27 years old
I first found out I had herpes when I went to the doctor because of some pain on my labia. He told me what it was and that there was nothing to be done about it but wait until it went away. He said lots of people had it and that I might get more attacks. I felt terrible. I felt used and contaminated. I caught it from a man I had been seeing for about a year. We were not exclusive with each other,

but we weren't promiscuous either. He told me after the fact. Needless to say, I was furious. Our 'relationship' didn't last much longer. All in all, it was a very low time for me. My relationship was finished, and in the bargain I had something that was painful, incurable and would be with me forever. I began making the rounds of doctors who all told me pretty much the same thing. I began to feel like a leper. Then I heard about lysine and I figured I might as well try it. It had been about six months since I first contracted herpes, and I had been getting an attack about once a month since then. So it couldn't get much worse. I was desperate enough that I took fairly 'large' doses. About four grams twice a day. That month the outbreak didn't come. I really didn't believe the lysine had worked, but I continued taking four grams twice a day and stayed away from chocolate (which I used to console myself with) and nuts. The second month came and still no attack. Then the third month came along and I got a little careless. I ate some chocolate, ran out of lysine, went on holiday and didn't get much sleep. I don't know if it was the chocolate, running out of lysine or running out of sleep, but I promptly got an attack. It's now been about three years since that time. I find that if I take lysine (about two grams a day), stay away from chocolate and nuts and don't go without sleep too often, I can pretty much control my outbreaks. I have been very cautious about getting into another relationship, but I feel that I'm about ready. I'm seeing a man now whom I care for very much. I remember how I felt about being deceived, so I decided to tell him I had herpes. He wasn't thrilled, but he has been very supportive. On a practical level he helps me a lot. Since we've been together, I've had only one outbreak and we both played detective to figure out why. A team effort. So, I guess you could say my life is back to 'normal' now. The only differences are that I'm much more aware of taking care of myself and more discriminating in my relationships.

Interview 2
Ted R., 23 years old
I'm a bachelor, and I used to have a very active social life. Every night I'd be out with someone else. I hardly ever went to bed alone and hardly ever took the same girl out twice. I'm not sure why I lived that way. It was just what most of the guys were doing – going to discos or bars at night. Seeing how often we could 'score'. Now that I look back, it seems pretty stupid, but at the time (this was about 2 years ago) it seemed that we were all trying to outdo each other. Well, one day I noticed that I'd got some sores. I'd had VD before, naturally, and so I wasn't real worried. I went to the doctor expecting the usual dose of penicillin but instead he tells me, 'Ted, penicillin won't work for this. You've got herpes.' In those days there wasn't the openness about herpes, so I didn't even know what it was. So I said, 'Well, give me whatever I need'. Then he said that there was nothing to do for herpes and it would just come back anyway. I asked him about the pain in my legs and he said that was part of it. 'Well, what can I do about it?' I asked. 'Nothing. Just keep the area dry and wear cotton underwear.' Nothing. I felt like I had been hit over the head. 'Well, what about going out with women?' I asked him. I guess the doctor thought he was real funny, because he said it was fine to go out with them, but just don't make love with them. Funny. I then went to about five other doctors to see what could be done and got about the same response (minus the jokes). Nothing. One doctor was pretty helpful. A woman doctor as a matter of fact. She said that herpes was very contagious just before, during and right after an outbreak, but that when all signs of the sores had gone and particularly if I used a condom I wouldn't have to worry about passing it on. She also told me about lysine and arginine and taking better care of myself.

During the time I was going from doctor to doctor, I had a lot of time to think about my lifestyle and how dumb it was, so by the time I got to this doctor, I was about ready to make some changes. I followed her suggestions about lysine and diet and taking better care of myself. I stayed away from sex for quite a while, maybe because I had had too much of it, maybe because of the herpes, I don't really know why. But it worked out fine because I met some really nice people and my whole social structure changed. I started 'dating'. I mean taking out women and getting to know them as friends. That was about a year ago. Now I can manage my herpes pretty well. Every now and then I get a flare up, but I know why. I'm still seeing a lot of different women, but on an entirely different basis. It sounds kind of odd, but I like my life a lot more now. I like me a lot more, too.

Interview 3
Kathy M., 16 years old
When people mention herpes, everybody always thinks of genital herpes, but I've got type 1 around the mouth. It's no fun either. I was getting these awful sores around my mouth every few weeks. First I'd get big blisters, then they'd break and the area would be all raw looking, then they'd scab over and I'd have these big ugly scabs. Just about the time they healed, the whole cycle would start all over again. I thought they were 'cold sores', but I couldn't work that out because I seldom get colds. I didn't know what they were from. I have this friend who has genital herpes and she was describing them to me and I made some kind of joke about how my sores and hers sounded alike, but just in different places. I didn't think any more about it until herpes started getting all this publicity. I read an article that described herpes 1, and it seemed to fit my situation. So, I went to a doctor who was running a herpes clinic in our area, and she confirmed that I did have herpes. It turns out that I probably got them at some family gathering or other. I remember one of my relatives having had 'cold sores' and our family is very close and

we're always sharing bites of things with each other and so on. I'd had these sores for about four years. This doctor asked if they seemed to get worse when I had been in the sun, and I remembered that they were always worse in the summer. I used to put all kinds of cream and stuff on them which only seemed to make them worse. She told me about lysine, about diet and getting enough rest. She told me not to put anything on the sores when I had them, but to use a good sun block when I was going to be in the sun (before I got them) and to wear a hat if I could. I rebelled at this for a while because it just didn't look cool. But then I started hearing about how the sun also causes wrinkles and skin cancer, so it seemed the best thing to do anyway. That was about six or eight months ago, and I haven't had an outbreak since. I may still get more attacks, but the important thing is that I know how to lessen the chances of getting an attack, I know how to take care of the sores if I do get them, and I know how to avoid passing them on.

Interview 4
George F., 45 years old
I found out that I had herpes about two months ago. I still feel like I'm living with a time bomb that may go off at any minute, but I suppose I'm feeling better than I did. I've been divorced a few years and I take women out from time to time, although my work keeps me too busy to get very involved. I'm not sure how or when I got it, I just remember feeling mildly ill and having pain in my buttocks and an irritation on my penis. So, I went to the doctor who told me that I had herpes. Well, I've read enough about herpes lately to know what it is and all I could say was 'Are you sure?'. He said he was and gave me some cream to put on it, telling me that it might help with the pain and cause the sores to go away faster; but it wouldn't be much good for future attacks. He gave me some reading to do and sent me on my way. One of the booklets he gave me outlined an approach to herpes that

involved stress management as well as lysine and diet. Since I had a problem with stress anyway, I decided that this would be the approach I would try. Because I work long hours, when I finally do get time to relax it's almost impossible for me. This booklet suggested getting some relaxation tapes, so I got a couple and finally found the one I like best. I listen to it every day and it's getting easier for me to relax. Of course, I'm taking lysine and cutting out arginine-rich foods too, but the thing that is making the difference is the stress management work. I'm sleeping a lot better, I work at a slower pace and yet seem to get a lot more done, and generally I'm beginning to feel less hassled. The time-bomb feeling is slowly beginning to go away, too. At first I felt that if I did anything wrong, I'd get an attack. If I worked too much or if I didn't get eight hours sleep, or if I ate something different. As time goes by, though, and I do my relaxation exercise every day (sometimes I even do them twice a day because I feel better afterwards), the feeling that something will erupt at any minute gets less and less.

I've only had one attack shortly after the first one. I was a nervous wreck at the time from finding out I had herpes, from a deadline at work, from just my general level of pressure. Since then I haven't had an attack. Although I may get one again sometime, I feel a lot more in control. One of the most important things about all of this is that my work is getting better. As I begin to relax with it a little more, it gets easier to do. Solutions that escaped me before are becoming obvious. Even more important, I'm enjoying it more, and for someone who devotes his whole life to his work, that's really great.

Interview 5
Diane N., 28 years old
I've had herpes since I was 23. I got it from my ex-fiancé. I thought we were only seeing each other, but I was wrong. But that's another story. In any case, after I was told that I

had herpes and got over the initial shock, I didn't think too much about it. I know that sounds unlikely, but after the attack went away, I didn't get another one for a long time, and so I really didn't think much about it. So, a few years went by and every now and then – about once a year – I'd get an attack. It was a nuisance, but since I wasn't going steadily with anyone (wasn't sexually active with anyone) it really wasn't a concern. Then about two years ago I met Hal. To make a long story short, after seeing each other for almost a year, we decided to get married. One day, I don't know why, the thought just popped into my head, 'You have herpes, you can't get married'. Then I really started to worry. I hadn't told Hal (I hadn't really even thought about it, it had been so long since my last attack) and I wasn't at all sure how he would take the news.

I rehearsed all kinds of ways to tell him in my mind. He knew that I had been engaged before, so that wouldn't be a surprise; but herpes was another matter. I tossed and turned at night wondering how to tell him and consequently got myself so het up that I brought on an attack. Hal was coming over that evening, so I prepared myself to tell him then, realizing that there was no 'perfectly right' time. Hal arrived and I began. I started by asking him if he knew what a cold sore was. He said yes and I told him that I sometimes got something like cold sores. He was appropriately sympathetic and changed the subject. I finally blurted out that instead of getting them on my lips, I got them genitally. He looked astonished at first, then really worried. I thought for sure that it was all over. Well, to shorten the story again, the reason he looked so worried was that I was in such a state. He asked me questions about getting it and how often I had attacks and what brought them on and so on. He said he didn't really know too much about herpes except that it was really contagious and what did I know about that. So, I told him what I knew and that there was no real risk if we were sensible about it. Then I will never forget what Hal said next. He told me that even if I did have herpes, it was only a small part of me and that he was marrying me for the person that I was – the total person. If that included herpes, then it did; and neither he nor I was to let it get out of proportion.

If I were to give anyone advice about how to feel about having herpes, I would tell them the same thing. You are a whole person, a unique blend of talents and attributes which is multifaceted and complex; and if anyone looks at you in a one-dimensional way and focuses on one element of your being (in this case herpes) you don't need that person in your life.

Epilogue: Diane and Hal were recently married.

Interview 6
Glenda P., 31 years old
I got herpes from my husband. Actually, he had told me that he had herpes before we were married, and we did what we could so I wouldn't catch it; but I suppose we were pretty unknowledgeable about it. Anyway, as the years went by we gained more and more knowledge about herpes and how to control it, so neither of us have outbreaks very often. For John, the vital thing is sleep and stress. As long as he gets enough sleep and does some sort of stress management, he's okay. For me, the important factor is chocolate and stress. If I don't have any chocolate and do some type of stress management, then I can control my outbreaks. So we have pretty good control over our attacks. The thing that has us both a little worried is that I'm pregnant. This can be risky. The main problem being that if I get too anxious about having an attack, it's likely that I will get one. So, it's something that I have to keep in mind, but not think about. So now I'm on a very careful programme. Absolutely no arginine-rich foods, lots of lysine-rich foods, rest and stress management techniques and two grams of lysine a day. My favourite

stress management techniques are either walking in the countryside or listening to a soothing record in absolute uninterrupted privacy for a half hour or so. Because John is also practising stress management, as well as being concerned for the baby and me, he really respects my need to be quiet and gives me a lot of support for it. So far so good. I feel really positive about this. I've gone for nine months before without an outbreak, and I feel I can do it again. It's rather like being in training. If I should get an attack, I know I can minimize it by tripling up my lysine dose and resting a little more. I think everything's going to be fine.

Epilogue: Two weeks ago, Glenda gave birth to a healthy, happy, eight-pound baby boy. She had no attack during her pregnancy. She feels it was her attitude that did it, along with her other preventive measures. 'I really think a neglected aspect to herpes control is to develop a positive attitude. Words like 'incurable' are so negative, it's hard to get around them. John and I are really convinced that a positive attitude is key in controlling herpes.'

Interview 7
David L., 30 years old
I'm not sure where I contracted herpes, or from whom. It was about six years ago and I was seeing several women. When I first found out I actually contemplated becoming a monk or something. I felt so ... contagious. There was a lot less discussion about herpes in those days. All I knew was that it was really communicable. There wasn't any ready information regarding any kind of treatments. I was left with a hopeless feeling and went into sort of a social decline. I didn't see anyone at all and, as I said, I actually contemplated some type of monastic life. However, I am really a gregarious person and I knew that that would be no solution. I began my 're-entry' into social life by dating only women with whom I had become friends. I know that

sounds like the way it should be anyway, but what I realized was that I (and I don't think I was unique) had been dating people that *looked* good to me, or who I was attracted to physically. Most of the time I hardly even knew them. So, I began by dating friends. Then, if the relationship progressed to a sexual stage and I told them about my herpes, I felt they would see me more as a person that they like with herpes, rather than someone with herpes that they hardly knew. If the relationship then progressed to the sexual stage (and sometimes it didn't), we were very careful not to have sex if I felt an attack coming on or had just recently got over one. As far as I know, in two years of dating no one has caught herpes from me. (Interestingly enough, on one or two occasions when I mentioned my herpes to a couple of women, they were really relieved because *they* had herpes too and were wondering how to tell *me*.) Eventually, one of these relationships became special and Sue and I were married. That was two years ago. She didn't have herpes when we were married and still doesn't. We are both careful about my herpes – not that it plays a central role in our lives, but Sue keeps chocolate and nuts out of the house. Although I don't take a maintenance dose of lysine, I do take four grams of lysine three times a day the *instant* I even *suspect* an outbreak brewing. Since I've been married, I've had only two attacks and they were more or less predictable. The lysine seems to really shorten the attacks I do get, although usually it prevents them altogether if I take it early enough. Although I take my herpes very seriously, it has become no more than a temporary inconvenience – one which I have learned to live with, one which helps me take better care of myself and one which I am very careful to keep to myself.

Interview 8
Laura P., 72 years old
I'm a widow and have just become a grandparent for the

fourth time. I was happily married to my husband, James, for nearly fifty years. When he died suddenly last year, I was shocked and really unable to function for some time. For about six months, I just got more and more depressed and really neglected my health. I didn't have any appetite, stopped my daily walks, lost weight and felt more and more fatigued. Friends and family tried to help, but I know they preferred to avoid me. I was pretty poor company. Even my dog began looking depressed. Eventually, my stomach began to really bother me and I landed in the hospital for tests. My doctor soon informed me I had a small ulcer. He said neither of us should be surprised because I had been under a great deal of emotional stress; and neglecting my physical health hadn't helped. He strongly recommended that I get some live-in help for a while, and start taking decent care of myself. Well, the pain I was having frightened me, so I decided to make an effort to follow his advice when I got home. The morning I was to be discharged from the hospital I noticed a tingling and burning in my genital area, but I tried to ignore it. But at home that night, I couldn't ignore it any longer. When I examined myself I couldn't believe it – I had about half a dozen red raw sores. It really frightened me, so I called my doctor at home and described the situation to him. He agreed to meet me at his office and do an examination. When he turned red and stammered after the examination, I couldn't imagine what was wrong. Then he told me I had herpes. Well, I knew all about herpes because my eighteen-year-old grandson had recently acquired it and had come to me for advice and consolation. I'm a retired biology professor and he trusted my professional opinion as well. So I had done my homework and together we had worked on his herpes problem – primarily by trying to improve his overall health.

But I still wasn't prepared for the emotional shock of discovering that I had it also. My first reaction was anger at whomever had given it to me. This was closely followed by feelings of betrayal. It seemed likely that James must have given it to me sometime during our marriage. This was really devastating to me since I had never believed that infidelity was possible for either of us.

Then I finally remembered a time when I had a passionate affair with a very charming fellow – more than fifty years ago. I vaguely recalled having some pain and soreness in the genital area. But in those days I was too young and embarrassed about my body to take a close look. I was only about nineteen at the time.

Well, the whole thing finally began to make sense. I had probably acquired herpes way back then and never had a recurrence. I am basically very healthy and work hard at staying that way. My system has always been strong. And it wasn't surprising that I would finally get a recurrence after months of grief and self-neglect. Even if I had caught it from James, chances are he had acquired it before our marriage. In any case, it really wasn't that important. We had loved each other.

I knew that I wouldn't have any future problems as soon as I got back on the right track and started taking care of my body.

10.
QUESTIONS AND ANSWERS

Q: I have herpes zoster. Can I beat it the same way as herpes 1 or 2?

A: Shingles is another common infection caused by a herpes virus called herpes zoster.[56] The herpes zoster virus is believed to be the same virus that causes chicken-pox, which usually occurs in children. In the United States, over eighty per cent of children have been infected with this herpes virus by the age of nine. In more tropical regions infection may occur at an older age. Chicken-pox is usually not very serious. However, it can develop into pneumonia and encephalitis (infection of the brain).

Because chicken-pox is so common, most people carry the herpes zoster in their bodies throughout their lives. It can become active again in the form of shingles. In Britain, shingles may occur at a rate of about three persons out of every 1,000 each year. In the United States, the rate may be 1 to 2 cases per 1,000 per year. This may not seem like much, but since shingles occurs more frequently in older people, it can become a major problem. In Britain, if you look at people who have lived to be eighty-five years old, half of them will have experienced at least one attack of shingles. Shingles is relatively rare in people under twenty years old. It becomes steadily more common from that point on. Like other herpes viruses, zoster is more dangerous in people whose immune systems are not functioning well – due to illness, or treatments with radiation or chemotherapy which suppress

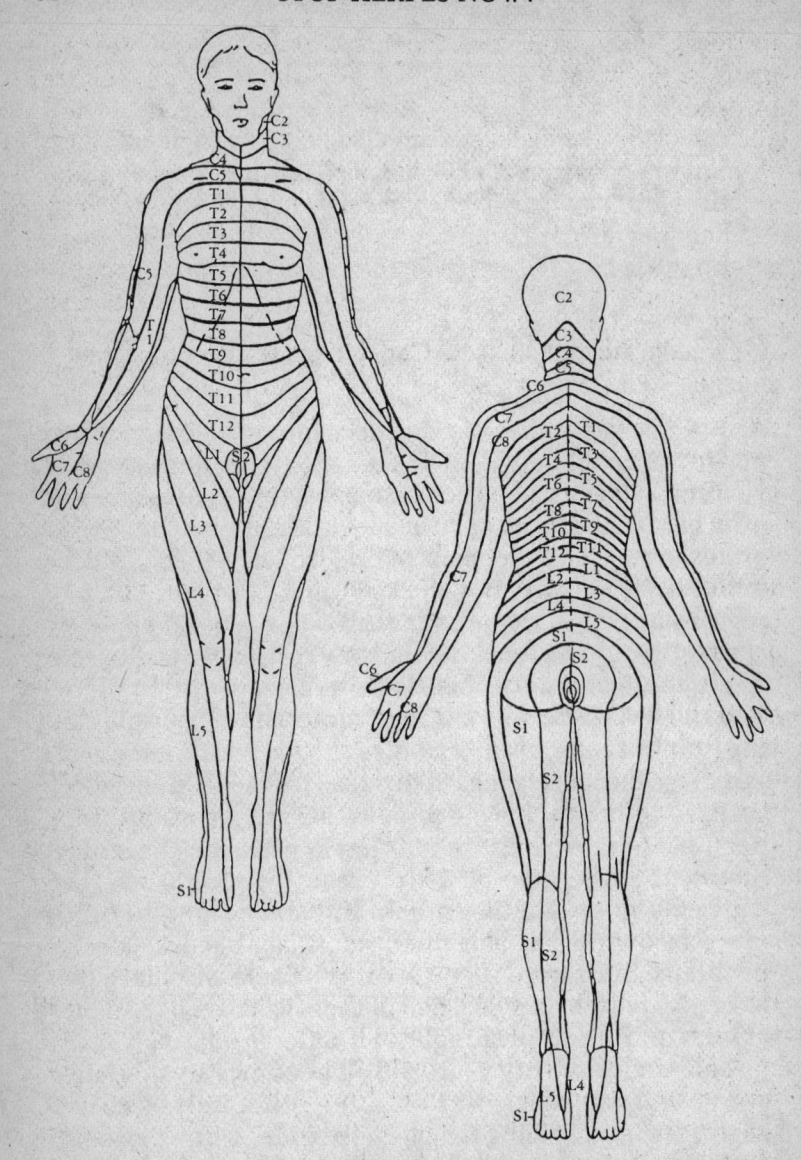

Figure 1: The Dematome.

normal immunity. However, there are now several promising treatments becoming available for these rare but serious cases, including gamma globulin, vaccination and intravenous acyclovir. It is also possible for a pregnant woman to transmit the infection to the foetus if she acquires chicken pox in the first six months of pregnancy – which may show up as congenital defects in the newborn or appear later as a recognizable infection in an infant.

Shingles usually begins as a tingling or burning sensation on a defined patch of skin, limited to an area called a 'dermatome'. (See Figure 1.) This is the skin which lies over one of the large nerves of the spinal cord. A pair of these so-called 'spinal nerves' is attached to the spinal cord every few inches, all the way from the neck to the tailbone. The herpes zoster virus presumably lies dormant at the base of one of these spinal nerves. When it becomes active, it migrates along a nerve to the overlying skin where fluid-filled blisters develop in a manner similar to herpes simplex. The attack is usually limited to the dermatome over a single spinal nerve either on the right or left. These blisters will often form a belt-like pattern from the backbone and wrapping around to the middle or the front of the body. This may happen on back, shoulder, hip or even the head and face. The blister stage gives way to scabs, and eventually heals. The sores often leave scars.

There may be considerable pain at all stages of the shingles attack and it can last for several weeks. In a small number of cases (about ten per cent) an individual may continue to experience pain in that same area for weeks or even years afterwards. Less than one per cent may have some residual paralysis of a nerve in the face called 'Bell's Palsy'.

We have less information about the possible effectiveness of nutritional approaches for people suffering from herpes zoster (shingles). There are some case reports of people with first attacks of herpes zoster who seem to recover more quickly and experience less pain when they adhere to the high lysine/low arginine dietary approach. The basic vitamin and mineral supplement programme is appropriate here as well. These measures may be helpful and can be added to any other treatment approach your physician may recommend.

Q. I have taken lysine for my herpes with no effect. Do some people not respond to lysine?

A. Some people do not seem to respond to taking l-lysine. This is possibly because they are either not taking a high enough dosage of lysine or are not doing anything else for their herpes, other than taking lysine pills. One must also avoid high-arginine foods, have a good basic diet, avoid sugar, fats, caffeine and alcohol, and try to reduce one's stress level. Also, be sure you are taking l-lysine (not plain 'lysine' or dl-lysine).

Q. Do I need to take vitamins to get rid of my herpes?

A. Everyone develops his or her own programme for herpes control – and vitamin and mineral supplements seem to help many people. The only thing that is really necessary is to take good care of yourself. If you have an unusually high quality diet with large amounts of garden-fresh fruits and vegetables, vitamin and mineral supplements may not be as important for you.

Q. I have herpes. How do I know when I am contagious?

A. Your sores are always contagious, and the contagious period may range from a few days before the sores actually appear and can continue for a few days after the sores are completely healed. There is some evidence that some people may shed herpes virus from their bodies even though they don't have an active attack. But don't over-react to this possibility. Just maintain commonsense personal hygiene and avoid contact when you think you may be getting an attack, during, and for a few days after an active attack.

Q. I am going with one man and I think he is seeing only me. We would like to be intimate, but I'm afraid of getting herpes. What should I do? P.S. I don't know if he has herpes or not.

A. Find out! Ask gently but directly. And give yourself extra protection by asking him to use a condom and you use a vaginal spermicide which contains nonoxynol-9. Sometimes a friend is offended or embarrassed by the question, but most people appreciate an opportunity to discuss it – whether they have herpes or not. And remember, if you have read this book, you are now an expert. You can supply correct information and help dispel fears born of lack of knowledge about the virus.

Q. Do I need to do everything you suggest to control herpes, or can I control my outbreaks with diet and lysine alone?

A. Some people seem to achieve excellent results with l-lysine and diet alone (don't forget to avoid arginine-rich foods). Others need to do more. Still others need to do *everything*. It really depends on your individual situation.

Q. I get cold sores regularly – but only at certain times. I get them in the summer and winter, but almost never in the spring. Can you tell me why and what to do about it?

A. Since you know what to expect, you are already a step ahead. First, be sure to avoid undue exposure to direct sunlight, especially in the summer. And watch out for winter holiday foods (usually rich in nuts and chocolates). Then try to figure out what makes spring a better time for you. Perhaps your diet is better or different somehow. Do you get more rest or recreation in the spring? You probably have a definite pattern, it's just a matter of identifying it.

Q. I've noticed that my glands get swollen when I have a herpes attack. Why is that, and is it dangerous?

A. This is a normal part of a herpes attack. Your body's immune system is working overtime. The glands are probably swollen lymph nodes which are like miniature militia – producing and processing white blood cells to help fight the infection. Herpes around the mouth causes glands in the neck to swell. Genital attacks cause enlarged glands in the groin. However, if the glands remain enlarged several weeks after the attack subsides, or if a gland gets extremely swollen and painful, check with your doctor.

Q. I've heard about a cream to put on herpes sores that makes them stop hurting and go away. What is it? Does it really work?

A. One herpes cream is called Acyclovir. It is a prescription medication which may help if this is your first herpes attack and if you start using it right away. You can probably get it from your doctor. The drawback of Acyclovir is that it is only helpful if you use it in the early stages of your first attack. It is not very helpful for a recurrent attack. Ice, zinc solution, povodone-iodine and aloe may all help with shortening the attack and reducing pain. There are many other creams available, some of which may contain ingredients to prevent infection, but most are less effective than the methods recommended here. So far, no one has developed a herpes 'cure', so be suspicious of any product that calls itself a cure.

Q. I have herpes, but I don't know where or how I got it and I feel terrible. I don't want to become involved with anybody or even get married. It seems as though I will never be able to lead a normal life. What can I do?

A. Be easy on yourself. Many people get herpes without any obvious source. Even genital herpes can be spread without sexual contact. Most people find that if you take care of yourself (good diet, l-lysine supplements, stress management, vitamins and minerals) you will get few or even no recurrent herpes attacks. And, over time, your body may increase its natural immunity to herpes so that the virus will stay quiescent. When you are ready to develop a close personal relationship with someone new, be open and discuss it with that person. You will probably be pleasantly surprised at how supportive the other person will be. If he or she is not supportive, you are probably much better off knowing that they are uncomfortable or unreasonable about the problem while it is still early in the relationship. And you are probably better off without them. Be open to a relationship, and possibly because of herpes, it will be stronger and more honest than it might have otherwise been.

Q. Lysine seems to help my herpes go away more quickly (or if I take it in time, sometimes I can prevent an attack altogether). What if I just took lysine all the time? How much should I take and are there any side-effects?

A. It depends on how often you get an attack. If it is once a month or more, you might try taking l-lysine (two or three 500mg tablets a day) for a few months. (Remember that lysine is more effective if taken between meals.) Also, *strictly* avoid arginine-rich foods. Then, when you have gone several months without an attack, taper the l-lysine down to nothing over a few weeks. Begin taking it again when you feel an attack coming on. (And don't forget to do your stress reduction exercises.) There are no known side-effects from taking l-lysine pills. The exception is the individual with a rare inherited disorder of metabolism which prevents them from digesting lysine normally. Check with your doctor if you have any doubts. Even so, if you feel ill after taking l-lysine (or any food or medicine for that matter), discontinue it.

Q. Does vitamin C help the lysine, or is it just good to take vitamin C for itself?

A. Many scientists believe that vitamin C should be taken as a vitamin supplement by everyone because we simply don't get enough in our foods, because our foods aren't fresh enough or are processed, which causes loss of vitamin C. A recent study showed that healthy people who took 2000mg of vitamin C a day had more active white blood cells (suggesting a more active immune system). For herpes, be sure you take bioflavonoids as well; this substance seems to make vitamin C work even more effectively. Vitamin C and lysine probably work independently of each other.

Q. I take my lysine with the rest of my vitamins – along with my meals. Someone told me I should take lysine by itself. Is this true?

A. Probably. Research on amino acid absorption in humans has shown that lysine is probably absorbed into the bloodstream more completely if you take it by itself – that is, without food or other substances. Vitamins almost always contain starches and amino acids or sugars, so it is best to take your vitamins and minerals with food for better absorption and to avoid indigestion.

Q. I noticed an increased discharge with my herpes. Does this mean they are in my vagina as well as on my labia?

A. Probably not. The increased discharge is not unusual. However, you may want your doctor to examine you during the early stages of an attack to give you exact information on the location of your sores. And if your discharge is unusually itchy, smelly, or irritating, get checked for a vaginal infection (which probably has nothing to do with your herpes). If you are a man, discharge from the penis is almost always a sign of a sexually transmitted infection (not herpes). Get checked at once.

Q. Do homosexual men run any special risks with herpes?

A. Homosexual men can transmit herpes as easily as heterosexual couples. In addition, if they engage in anal sex, they may acquire herpes in the rectum which causes a great deal of pain and sometimes infection and bleeding as well. If this condition occurs, it should be monitored by a doctor.

Q. I got herpes several years ago from my husband. Since my divorce, my partners now are exclusively the same sex (women). Do I need to worry about giving them herpes?

A. The same question of transferring the herpes virus applies to any sexual partner. Any skin-to-skin contact can transmit herpes when sores are present. Open sores should not be touched and basic hygiene should be observed. Generally speaking, because penis/vagina contact is non-existent, unless you were to transmit the virus manually, contagion would not be as likely.

Q. I have 'cold sores' (type 1), and I'm worried about passing them on to the rest of my family. What's the best way to prevent this?

A. Most forms of Herpes Simplex virus 1 are passed via kissing. The best way to avoid infecting your family is to avoid skin-to-skin contact if there is any sign of a herpes sore (either the pre-eruption tingling or the post-eruption scabbing). Good basic hygiene (hand washing, not sharing facecloths, etc., as well as no sharing of glasses or utensils) will keep the virus from spreading.

Q. I've heard that stress can bring on a recurrence of herpes. Is this true? I'm usually quite relaxed, yet I get recurrent attacks. What else brings on an attack?

A. As you know, once a person has the virus it remains in the ganglia until it is reactivated. Several things trigger a recurrent infection: fever, respiratory infections or any serious illness, emotional strain or upset, hormonal changes with menstruation, exposure to excessive sun, lack of sleep, poor nutrition (eating high-arginine foods and 'empty calories'), and friction on a body area from tight clothes.

Q. I might have herpes but I'm not sure. How would I know?

A. The surest way, of course, is to check with your doctor. It is best to go when there is an actual sore to be checked. There are other sexually-transmitted diseases that could be confused with herpes, so to be absolutely sure it is best to have a doctor check. In general, the symptoms of herpes are a tingling or burning, followed by a greatly increased sensitivity, not only in the area where the sores develop, but the surrounding area as well. Eventually, one or more small fluid-filled sores will form that resemble blisters. Other symptoms (particularly with a first occurrence) are fever, headache and loss of energy. Recurring outbreaks – if there are any (and sometimes there are not) – are usually shorter and less severe than the first.

Q. I have genital herpes and am almost positive that I did not get it from sexual contact. Is there another way I could have possibly caught it?

A. Laboratory studies show that the herpes virus may be able to live for up to a day on surfaces such as toilet seats. It is not very likely that there would be enough living viruses left after this length of time to transmit the disease. However, since it is a *possibility*, common sense would suggest using paper on toilet seats before sitting or assuming a half-standing posture and not touch the toilet seat at all. Moist cloth has also been found to harbour the virus, so that it is important for persons with active herpes to use separate towels, facecloths, underwear, bathing suits, etc. In swimming pools and saunas the chemicals and heat usually kill the viruses while in the water. It is possible that you picked up the virus in one of the above ways, but it isn't very likely.

Q. Can herpes affect your sexual desire? A few months ago I got herpes from my husband (who later admitted he was having an affair). I was very angry with him for a while, but we are both trying to keep our marriage together. I feel that our relationship is stronger than ever, but I have absolutely no sexual interest in him, and we are both very upset.

A. Herpes cannot reduce libido directly, but it certainly can have a powerful psychological effect on a couple – especially when an outside sexual relationship is involved. First, be patient with yourself. It has only been a few months, and you may need more time. Second, get some professional counselling if possible – both for yourself privately and as a couple if possible. And be sure to select someone with experience and professional training in sexual counselling. (Many psychotherapists, counsellors, ministers, psychologists, doctors, and other professionals who do general counselling are *not* qualified to handle sexual problems.) The problem here seems to be one of trust as well as one of herpes.

Q. I'm worried that my cold sores on my upper lip are spreading. I hadn't had an attack for five years. Then last month I got a sudden attack with twice as many sores as I ever had before. I'm worried. I have been awfully sick from the flu, and I've been working overtime. Could that really make a difference?

A. Yes! Our patients tell us over and over again that overwork and illness are two of the most common reasons for getting a herpes attack. It is not unusual for sores to appear in new locations, especially when you are highly stressed. However, the 'spread' is nearly always limited to a few new sores, close to the old ones. And it doesn't mean that you will necessarily get more attacks or more spreading. (It probably does mean that your immune system isn't in very good shape, and you need to start taking better care of yourself.) Very rarely, herpes will spread to many parts of the body. But this invariably happens to people who are very ill (and often hospitalized) and whose immune systems are severely impaired.

11.
THE HERPES HANDBOOK

To Prevent Communicating Herpes To Anyone Else:

1. Avoid touching your herpes sore with any object which may be used by someone else (for example, facecloth, eating utensils, etc.).

2. Do not allow anyone else to come in contact with your sores through direct skin-to-skin contact.

3. If you have genital herpes, avoid intercourse (or any other form of genital contact) as soon as you suspect an attack may be coming on, during the attack, and for a few days after the sores have healed. For extra safety, use a condom and a vaginal spermicide (containing nonoxynol-9) whenever possible – even though you have no active sores.

4. Follow commonsense precautions in your personal hygiene: wash your hands when awakening and after touching the area around your sores.

To Keep From Getting Herpes Yourself:

1. Avoid touching skin sores on another person – especially when they are around the mouth and genitals.

2. Don't share facecloths, towels, eating utensils, intimate clothing, etc., with another person.

3. Don't be shy – ask your new friend about his or her

health *before* you have intercourse. For extra safety, use a condom and vaginal spermicide.

4. Help your body resist infection from herpes – use good nutrition, exercise, and conscious stress reduction techniques to keep your immune system in top condition.

If You Have Had Herpes In The Past, How To Prevent Further Outbreaks:

1. Identify and try to avoid the stresses which are most likely to bring on an attack (fatigue, mental stress, poor nutrition, over-indulging in alcohol, sugar, etc.).

2. Stimulate your immune system with an optimal diet (fresh, unprocessed foods, reduce fat and sugar intake).

3. Suppress herpes virus growth with high l-lysine intake (use lysine-rich foods and l-lysine pill supplements taken one hour before or after meals). Dose range is one 500mg tablet three to four times a day. Avoid arginine-rich foods (*all* nuts, seeds and chocolate).

4. Keep your stress level as low as possible.

5. Use a balanced vitamin and mineral supplement (especially vitamin C, bioflavonoids, zinc, B complex) to stimulate your immune system.

If You Have Had Herpes In The Past, And Think You Are Getting An Outbreak:

1. Step up your l-lysine intake with lysine-rich foods and tablets. Take two 500mg tablets four times a day.

2. Get lots of rest.

3. *Rigidly* avoid arginine-rich foods (*all* nuts, seeds, chocolate).

4. Avoid sugar, fats, caffeine (coffee, tea, colas) and alcohol.

5. Apply ice to the area of skin where you feel the sores are beginning to develop. Apply continuously for thirty to sixty minutes (do not freeze skin).

6. Begin vitamin and mineral supplements if you have not already done so.

7. Begin relaxation exercises immediately and do them for ten to thirty minutes each day.

8. Include some positive imaging with your relaxation throughout the day.

If You Get An Outbreak:

1. Do all of the above.

2. After applying ice to the sores, apply a clean compress soaked in a solution of zinc sulphate (.025% or .05% in water) to the sores for about ten minutes.

3. Follow the zinc solution with an application of 10% povidone-iodine solution. Use a cotton-tipped applicator to paint solution gently on sores.

4. Repeat povidone-iodine application four times a day.

5. Alternatively (if you are allergic to iodine or you would like an alternative), apply pure aloe gel to the sores four times a day. (Aloe gel is the sap of the aloe plant, and greatly aids in healing skin lesions.)

6. Repeat ice application once more in twenty-four hours if pain has not subsided.

7. Maintain careful handwashing precautions and be especially careful to avoid touching your eyes (this includes contact lenses or anything that goes in the eye).

Note: If zinc, povidone-iodine solution or aloe appears to make your sores worse, discontinue at once. You may have an allergic reaction. See your doctor if the sores do not improve in a few days or if they seem to spread or appear infected.

Take good care of yourself and herpes will not be a problem for you.

APPENDIX

The food lists found in Tables 2 and 3 were compiled as follows:
1. Amino acid content per serving was obtained from: 'Amino Acid Content of Foods', *FAO Nutritional Studies*, No.24, FAO, Rome, 1970; and *Nutrition Almanac*, Nutrition Search, Inc., McGraw-Hill Book Co., New York, London, 1975.

2. Excess lysine or excess arginine was calculated using molar ratios in each food.* Molar ratios (ratio of number of lysine molecules to number of arginine molecules in a food) were used rather than weight ratios (milligrams) since it has been shown that the amount of an amino acid absorbed across the intestine is proportional to the molar ratios of the amino acids composition of the food eaten (see Leathem, J. H., (ed.), *Protein Nutrition and Free Amino Acid Patterns*, Rutgers University Press, New Jersey, 1968).

3. Lysine excess or deficiency (shown by molar ratios) were then converted to weight (in milligrams) of lysine for easy interpretation in Tables 2 and 3.

*Eggs have been removed from the lysine excess list because absorption studies show that eggs produce a lowering of lysine in the blood, even though they contain a slight lysine excess.

REFERENCES

1. Leo, John. 'The New Scarlet Letter'. *Time Magazine*, August 2, 1982: 62-69.
2. Adour, K. K., et al. 'Meniere's disease as a form of cranial polyganglionitis'. *Laryngoscope*, 1980, 90(3):392-8.
3. Adour, K. K., et al. 'Herpes simplex polyganglionitis'. Otolaryngol. *Head Neck Surg.*, 1980, 88(3) : 270-4.
4. Warren, K. G., et al. 'Herpes simplex virus latency in patients with multiple sclerosis'. *IARC Sci. Publ.*, 1978, 24(2) : 765-8.
5. Curry, S. S. 'Cutaneous herpes simplex infections and their treatment.' *Cutis*, 1980, 26(1) : 41-58.
6. Terezhalmy, G. T., et al. 'The use of water soluble bioflavonoid-ascorbic acid complex in the treatment of recurrent herpes labialis'. *Oral Surgery*, 1978, 45(1) : 56.
7. Guinan, M., et al., 'Course of untreated recurrent genital herpes simplex infection in 27 women'. *New Eng. J. Med.*, 1981, 304(13) : 759-64.
8. Adam, E., et al., 'Asymptomatic virus shedding after herpes genitalis'. *Am. J. Obstet. Gynecol.*, 1980, 137(7) : 827-30.
9. Tantivanich, S., & Tharavanij, S., 'Prevalence of genital herpes virus infection in Thai women'. *Southeast Asian J. Trop. Med. Public Health*, 1980, 11(1) : 126-30.
10. Reeves, W. C., et al., 'Risk of recurrence after first episodes of genital herpes'. *New Eng. J. Med.*, 1981, 305(6) : 315-19.
11. Hirsch, M. S., & Schooley, R. T., 'Treatment of herpes virus infections. Parts 1 & 2.' *New Eng. J. Med.*, 1983; 309(16) : 963-70, and 309 (17) : 1034-39.
12. Zur Hansen, H., 'Human genital cancer: synergism between a virus infection and initiating events'. *Lancet*, 1982, 2(8312) : 1370-2.

13. Curole, D. N. 'Managing genital herpes virus infection: the state of the art'. *Consultant*, June, 1981, 47-53.
14. Cabral, G. A., et al. 'A herpes virus antigen in human premalignant and malignant cervical biopses and explants'. *Am. J. Obstet. Gynecol.*, 1983, 145(1) : 79-83.
15. Kaufman, R., et al., 'Herpes virus-induced antigens in squamous-cell carcinoma in situ of the vulva'. *New Eng. J. Med.*, 1981, 305(9) : 483-88.
16. Kibrick, S., 'Herpes simplex at term'. *J. Am. Med. Assoc.*, 1980, 243(2) : 157-60.
17. Boehm, F. H., et al., 'Management of genital herpes virus infection occurring during pregnancy'. *Am. J. Obstet. Gynecol.*, 1981, 141(7) : 735-40.
18. Harger, J. H., et al., 'Characteristics and management of pregnancy in women with genital herpes simplex virus infection'. *Am. J. Obstet. Gynecol.*, 1983, 145(7) : 784-91.
19. Kagan, C., 'Herpes Update II'. *Saturday Evening Post*, Oct. 1982, 39-40.
20. Montefiore, D., et al. 'Herpes virus type 2 infection in Ibadan. Problem of non-venereal transmission'. *British J. Venereal Dis.*, 1980, 56(1) : 49-53.
21. Anon. 'Single nutrient effects on immunologic functions. *The Helper* (American Social Health Assoc.), 1981, 3(2): 6-8.
22. Pearson, H. E., et al., 'Effect of certain amino acids and related compounds on propogation of mouse encephalo-myelitis virus'. *Proc. Soc. Exp. Biol. Med.*, 1952, 70 : 409-11.
23. Tankersley, R., 'Amino acid requirements of herpes simplex virus in human cells.' *J. Bact.*, 1964, 87 : 609-13.
24. Griffith, R. S., et. al., 'Relation of arginine-lysine antagonism to herpes simplex growth in tissue culture'. *Exp. Chemo.*, 1981, 27 : 209-13.
25. Griffith, R. S., et al., 'A multicentered study of lysine therapy in herpes simplex infection'. *Dermatologia*, 1978, 156 : 257-267.
26. Lerner, J., *A Review of Amino Acid Transport Processes in Animal Cells and Tissues*. University of Maine at Orono Press, Orono, Maine 1978.
27. Leathem, J. H. (ed.), *Protein Nutrition and Free Amino Acid Patterns*. Rutgers University Press, New Brunswick, N.J., 1968.

28. Murray, M. J., et al.,'Molluscum contagiosum and herpes simplex in Maasai pastoralists; refeeding activation of virus infection following famine'. *Transactions Royal Society Tropical Medicine Hygiene*, 1980, 74(3) : 371-4.
29. Kagan, C., 'Lysine Therapy for herpes simplex'. *Lancet*, 1974, 1 : 137.
30. Milman N., et al., 'Lysine prophylaxism in recurrent herpes simplex labialis: a double blind, controlled crossover study'. *Act. Dermat. Venereolog.* (Stockholm), 1980, 60(1) : 85-87.
31. Milman, N., et al., 'Failure of lysine treatment in recurrent herpes simplex labialis'. *Lancet*, October 28, 1978 : 942.
32. Blank, H., & DiGiovanna, J., *Failure of lysine in the treatment and prophylaxis of frequently recurrent herpes simplex infection.* University of Miami School of Medicine, Miami. (Ms. in Press.)
33. U.S. F.D.A. Department of Health & Human Services. 'Orally administered drug products for the treatment of fever blisters'. *Federal Register*, January 5, 1982, p.508.
34. Anon. 'Help membership HSV Survey Research Project Results'. *The Helper* (American Social Health Assoc.), 1981, 3(2) : 1-5.
35. SerVaas, C., 'Does l-lysine stop herpes? *Sat. Eve. Post.*, July/August 1982 : 28.
36. SerVaas, C., 'Herpes Update'. *Sat. Eve. Post*, September, 1982 : 60.
37. Corey, L., et al., 'A trial of topical Acyclovir in genital herpes simplex virus infections'. *New Eng. J. Med.*, 1982, 306(22) : 1313-9.
38. Anon., 'Topical Acyclovir for herpes simplex'. *The Medical Letter*, 1982. 24(611) : 55-56.
39. Balfour, H., et al., 'Acyclovir halts progression of herpes zoster in immunocompromised patients'. *New Eng. J. Med.*, 1983, 308(24) : 1447-48.
40. Crumpacker, C. S., et. al., 'Resistance to antiviral drugs of herpes simplex virus isolated from a patient treated with Acyclovir'. *New Eng. J. Med.*, 1982, 306(6) : 343-46.
41. Buge, A., et al., 'Isoprinosine in treatment of acute viral encephalitis'. *Lancet*, September 29, 1979 : 691.
42. Wickett, W., Jr., *Herpes: Cause and control.* Pinnacle Books, Inc., New York, 1982.

43. Bradshaw, L. J., et al., 'Immunological and clinical studies on herpes simplex patients treated with inosiplex'. *4th Int. Cong. Immunology*, Paris, France, July 21-26, 1980.
44. Wallin J., et al., 'Therapeutic efficacy of trisodium phosphonoformate in treatment of recurrent herpes labialis'. In: Nahmias, A. J., et al., eds. *The Human Herpes Virus*. Elsevier Press, New York, 1981 : 681.
45. Helgstrand, E., et al., 'Trisodium phosphoroformate, a new antiviral compound'. *Science*, 1976, 201 : 819-21.
46. Skinner, G. R., et al., 'Preparation and immunogenicity of vaccine Ac NFUI (S-) MRC towards the prevention of herpes genitalis'. *British J. Vener. Dis.*, 1982, 58(6) : 381-6.
47. Klein, R. J., 'Effect of immune serum on the establishment of herpes simplex virus infection in trigeminal ganglia of hairless mice'. *J. Gen. Virol.*, 1980, 49(2) : 401-5.
48. Zimmerman, D. R., 'Self treatment of cold sores with ice'. *The Lancet*, 1978, 2 : 1260.
49. Danziger, S., 'Ice packs for cold sores'. *The Lancet*, 1978, 1 : 103.
50. Wahba, A., 'Topical application of zinc-solutions'. *Acta. Derm. Venereol.*, (Stockholm), 1980, 60(2) : 175-77.
51. Brody, I., 'Topical treatment of recurrent herpes simplex and post-herpetic erythema multiforme with low concentrations of zinc sulphate solution'. *British J. Derm.*, 1981, 104(2) : 191-4.
52. Friedrich, E. G., Jr., and Mosukawa, T. 'The effect of povidone-iodine on herpes genitalis'. *Obstet. Gynecol.*, 1975, 45 : 337.
53. Bullough, J., 'Use of povidone-iodine alcoholic solution in the treatment of herpes genitalis'. *Current Med. Res. & Opinion*, 1979, 6(3) : 175-77.
54. Judson, M. D., 'Condoms prove effective against herpes, chlamydia'. *Contraceptive Technology Update*. 1983, 4(11) : 129-40.
55. Singh, B., et al., 'Virucidal effect of certain chemical contraceptives on type 2 herpes virus'. *Am. J. Obstet. Gynecol.*, 1976, 126 : 422-25.
56. Weller, T. H., 'Varicella and herpes zoster, Parts 1 and 2.' *New Engl. J. Med.* 1983, 309(22) : 1361-68, and 309(23) : 1434-40.

INDEX

Acyclovir, 56, 57, 89, 92
'adrenalin addicts', 45
aloe gel, 59, 101
Amino Acid Content of Foods, 41
animal protein, 41
anti-herpes vaccines, 58
    Lepine, 59
    Lupidon G, 58
    Lupidon H, 58
arginine, 22, 31, 32
    -rich foods, 13, 34, 40, 100

'Bell's Palsy', 89
bioflavonoids, 28, 94
bromovinyldeoxyuridine (BVDU), 58

caring for herpes sores, 59-61
cervix, 13
    cancer of, 18
chicken pox, 87
cold sores, 9, 12, 54, 63, 78, 91, 96, 98
common cold, 17
contagious period, 90
contraceptives, use of, 63, 91, 99
cytomegalovirus (CMV), 9

deoxyribonucleic acid (DNA), 9, 32, 56
dermatome, 88, 89
diagnosis of herpes, 16, 96, 97

encephalitis, 18, 57, 87
eye infections, 18, 57

fibre, in diet, 24
'fight or flight' reaction, 44
Food and Agricultural Organization, 41

genital herpes, 9, 13, 64, 97
    (see also herpes simplex type 2)
glands, swollen, 92

herpes culture tests, 16, 17
herpes simplex, type 1, 9, 12
    type 2, 9, 13
    virus (HSV), 9
herpes zoster, 9, 57, 87-90
high-fibre/low-fat diet, 25
homosexuality, 95
hygiene, personal, 15

Idoxuridine, 58

immune system, 11, 12, 22, 43, 68, 72
impetigo, 54
infants, herpes infections in, 19, 33
  prevention of infection in, 20
interferon, 58
Isoprinosine, 58

labia, 13
libido, 98
location of herpes sores, 13-15
lymph nodes, swollen, 14, 92
lysine, 22, 31, 32
  l-lysine, 38, 39, 41, 90, 93, 94, 100

meningitis, 18
mineral supplement, 27, 90

oral sex, 15

Pap smear test, 17, 18
penis, 14
phosphonoformate, 58
'placebo effect', 21, 37, 69
positive thinking, 71, 74
povidone-iodine solution, 60, 101
pregnancy, herpes attacks during, 19, 82-83

relaxation techniques, 46-50, 72, 73

Saturday Evening Post, The (report in), 36-37

shingles (see herpes zoster)
Simonton, Dr Carl, 71
Statistics of herpes sufferers, 12, 14
stress, as trigger factor, 11, 22, 43, 96
  evaluation key, 51-53
  management skills, 22, 44, 80
sun, exposure to, 13
support groups, 65, 75
swelling and pain, reduction of, 59

Trifluorothymidine, 58
trigger factors, 11

United States Federal Drug Administration, 35
urethra, 13

vaginal secretions, 60, 95
varicella zoster virus (VZV), 9
vesicles (blisters), 13
vidabine, 57
vitamin C, 28, 94
vitamin supplement, 27, 90

zinc sulphate solution, 59, 101